EYE ON I

S.B. Sunit

Eye on I
ISBN 978-93-5346-290-1
Philosophy / Mind & Body

Published by Sunit A. Bhatewara
www.DrSunit.com
PO Box 1908, Kothrud, Pune 411038 India

SUNIT

Printed in India

To

the curious seeker

Index

Diacritical Marks for Sanskrit

a is like the a in sofa

ā is like the a in father

i is like the i in tin

ī is like the i in pique

u is like the u in put

ū is like the u in rune

ṛ is like the re in fibre

ḷ is like the le in cable

e is like the ei in rein

ai is like the ai in aisle

o is like the o in opal

au is like the ou in out

c is like the ch in chuck

g is a hard g as in good

ṅ or *ṁ* is a guttural nasal, like the ng in ringing

ś or ṣ may both be pronounced as English sh

jñ can be pronounced as nny, or dny, or gy

A note to the reader

If you picked up this book and are reading this, this book is certainly meant for you!

Have you ever wondered, what is this thing that we call "I"? Have you ever reflected on the nature of your mind and its patterns and felt the curiosity to dive deeper? If so, this book will speak to you.

India has given to the world some extraordinary luminaries. This book explores six of these personalities – three from the ancient times: Ādi Śaṅkaracārya, Buddha, and Mahāvīra and three modern: Ramana Maharshi, Sri Aurobindo and J. Krishnamurti.

Although the book does investigate their philosophies, it also has a very pragmatic purpose. I have referred to the key theoretical concepts of each of these thinkers, but with a very clear applied focus on Self-realisation. The theme of this work does not in the slightest veer away from the key focus area of Self. What is self? Who are we? And how do we come to totally understand the true nature of our existence?

We look at the potent teachings of these six incredible masters from India and try to not only make sense of the meaning of their teachings but also critically analyse and compare what are seemingly opposite views. Finally we arrive at a synthesis that creates a holistic understanding of the nature of self and ways to realise it.

The book begins with a broad overview of the theories of self from all the prominent philosophies from the West and the

East--from Socrates to Nietzsche, and from Vedic- Upanishadic *darshanas* to Charvakas. In later chapters we dive deep into the rich philosophies and teachings of the select thinkers that are central to this work.

The book brings to you the rich wealth of knowledge which flourished in this land of India for a few thousand years and spread across the world, inspiring millions till date to look inwards and create a life which is truly fulfilling, meaningful and freeing.

The words here form the logical framework. The invitation to the reader is to go through it, understand it and finally transcend it by attaining the true perception of reality, which will certainly be not limited by these or any words.

I express my gratitude to the written word and invite you on this journey with me.

S.B. Sunit

Introduction

In the last few centuries science has made tremendous progress in understanding the universe. There exists today a great deal of knowledge related to the objects contained in the world. However, the same cannot be said about our attempts at understanding the subject and subjectivity. The disciplines of psychology, anthropology and sociology have attempted to understand the person, or the subject, who is perhaps at the centre of life on this planet. For example, personality psychology tries to define the self based on the concept of personality rather than merely focusing on certain states and traits of a person. Yet, I discovered in my doctoral studies that the concept of personality is very limited in understanding the self. It was on this background that the present work was initiated.

Philosophy as a discipline investigates the whole concept of self. In particular, Indian philosophy encompasses rich traditions which have elaborated on theories of self and practices of self-realisation. This book focuses on key thinkers from ancient and modern India with regards to their theories of self and self-realisation. The thinkers covered in this book have been selected on account of the multiplicity of philosophical positions they hold and the traditions they represent. Śaṅkara based his works on the Upaniṣads of the orthodox Vedic tradition, whereas Buddha and Mahāvīra hail from the unorthodox *śramaṇa* traditions. These can be seen as three major thinkers, whose individual teachings have led to what we see today as major philosophies and religions arising from ancient India.

In modern times, particularly the twentieth century, we saw some spiritual personalities emerging from India who still continue to influence a vast majority of seekers and scholars with their distinct approach to the concepts of self and self-realisation. Again the selection of these thinkers for this book is influenced by the distinct approaches they take in elaborating their thoughts. Ramana Maharshi advocates Advaita Vedānta and teaches the supremacy of the path of self-enquiry in his own way. Krishnamurti, on the other hand, denies all traditions and schools of philosophy and religion, and approaches the question of truth by stating that 'truth is a pathless land'. Aurobindo contrastingly begins his theory of integral yoga based on the Vedas and Upaniṣads, but takes it to some completely new paradigms, never seen in Indian traditions before: these pertain to the evolution of mankind to a new race of superhuman.

This book describes, critically compares and finally synthesises these approaches towards self and self - realisation. Specifically:

- Different dimensions of self-realisation put forth by specific ancient and modern Indian philosophers
- Metaphysical reasons that were behind the unique approaches taken by these philosophers
- Analysis of the phenomenon of self-realisation on empirical grounds with reference to affective, cognitive and behavioural functions.
- Synthesis of these approaches to self-realisation which provides a meaningful and comprehensive understanding

Methodology

Thinkers vs. Systems

This book is based on thinkers and not the systems. Thus, it is not a study of Advaita Vedānta, Jainism or Buddhism. Rather it is based on teachings of Śaṅkara, Buddha and Mahāvīra. As mentioned above, the teachings of these thinkers have influenced various schools of thought and sects and sub sects with their individual interpretations of the original teachings. In the process, a vast body of texts carrying numerous theories have emerged, often with opposing views--not only of systems from different traditions, but also those of different interpreters of their own traditions. Thus, this book avoids the philosophical debate amongst the systems by focusing on the original canonical texts, which are considered the closest possible narrations of the selected thinkers' actual teachings.

References

References have been taken from the primary sources. This becomes much easier in the cases of modern thinkers, as technology has made it possible to record and authenticate the originality of the material coming from them. Unfortunately, the same cannot be said about the ancient thinkers. Researchers do not deny the possibility of erroneously attributing certain works to these ancient thinkers. However, there are certain primary texts which are undoubtedly the closest that researchers can get to the original teachings, and such sources provide the vast majority of reference points for this research.

Order

The order in which the ancient thinkers are presented is not chronological. Although Śaṅkara's works came centuries after those of Buddha and Mahāvīra, his work is presented first. This is for two reasons; firstly, Śaṅkara's is an orthodox system in which he bases his work on ancient Vedic texts which existed before both Buddha and Mahāvīra. Neither Buddha nor Mahāvīra base their teaching on any such system or texts. Furthermore, to do proper justice to the narration and discussion of each theory, the order of theories presented moves from monistic to multifaceted. To elaborate, Śaṅkara's is a monistic theory, and Buddha, in his own way, denies any permanent substance, whereas, in Mahāvīra's theory, we find place for both permanent and transitory elements. Moreover, Mahavira's Anekāntavāda model permits the accommodation of various apparently contradictory theories. Hence, Mahāvīra's dualistic or, in some ways, pluralistic theory is discussed last in the series of ancient Indian thinkers. The modern thinkers studied here were contemporaries. Due to Ramana's adherence to the Advaita philosophy and its links to the ancient Vedic texts, his theory is presented first. Krishnamurti's purely unorthodox theory is presented at the end.

Sanskrit & Prakrit Terms

Various Sanskrit and Prakrit terms appear while studying the ancient thinkers. All such terms have been written with appropriate diacritical marks. Most of the Pali and Ardhamagadhi terms of Buddha and Mahāvīra respectively, have been translated in Sanskrit for uniformity and convenience.

Definitions

The meaning of the terms self and self-realisation considered in this book also needs to be defined at the outset. Although a detailed discussion of these concepts will follow in the chapters ahead, a brief outline is given here, in order to clarify the scope and the context of the book.

Self

Here the common-sense meaning of 'self' is employed, which is general subjectivity; the 'I' as experienced by all humans in daily life. This self, (the empirical 'self' rather than the metaphysical 'Self') is denoted by the first person pronoun 'I' in all languages. Thus, the reference to self in this research is from the standpoint of the empirically experienced self.

Various philosophers studied in this book have categorically different conceptions of self, including some denying its existence. These conceptions of self can be regarded as different answers to the question regarding the true (metaphysical) nature of this empirical self. So although the Buddha is said to have denied the metaphysical self, no one has denied the experience of everyday self. They may call it illusion but there are definite references to this self. It is this self that is the centre of the present research.

Self-realisation

When the true nature of such self (including its presence, as illusion or *skandha*, or absence) as explained above, is realised, this process and phenomenon is called self-realisation. The term self-realisation does fit well in the Vedic and Jain traditions, however it can attract certain criticism in the context of Buddha's teachings. As Buddha denied the existence of self, one may question how self-realisation is possible? Here again I would like to point out, for lack of a better alternative, that the common term 'self-realisation' is used to denote the process and phenomena in which the individual realises the truth about him or herself. Although this brief note may or may not suffice here, the detailed critical discussion in the following chapters will clarify the meaning and the implication of self - realisation in different theories.

Review

"Love for the truth", the literal meaning of the word philosophy, symbolises humanity's quest for understanding--making sense of and finding meaning in what one sees and experiences. This quest is not new to mankind, although it has taken varied forms. Consequently it has also had varied effects on man's understanding of himself and the world, thereby creating diverse cultures and societies. Furthermore, as Foucault may argue, this is essentially the knowledge (which Foucault closely links with power) that creates subjects and subjectivity.

Man's quest to understand his existence as a whole is an endeavour which includes metaphysical[1] and epistemological[2] approaches. As a natural outcome of his quest, he eventually embarks upon a fundamental, self-reflective question: 'Who am I?'. Now the knower himself is under question.

What follows is a brief survey of different conceptions of self as presented by important thinkers/systems from Western and Indian schools. Against that background, the theme of this book and its scope will be introduced. It should, however, be noted that the overview of the prominent Eastern and Western views on Self is by no means exhaustive. There are a number of prominent philosophers and schools which I have referred to in the following two chapters. This creates a background for the understanding of varied approaches of looking at Self from diverse chronological and geographic standpoints. While an attempt is made to include most of the significant views, it is beyond the scope of this book to include every single such theory. Once again, the purpose of the

---

1   Metaphysics explores the fundamental questions, including the nature of concepts like being, existence, and reality.
2   Epistemology addresses such questions as "What does it mean to say that we know something? "How do we know that we know?

following two chapters is to paint the canvas for the background of various philosophical standpoints before we dive deep into looking closely and critically at the views of the select six Indian thinkers.

Chapter 1

Self in the West

Socrates

One can discern the beginnings of enquiry into the nature of self in Plato's account of some of the Socratic dialogues. In a particular dialogue with Alcibiades, Socrates asks Alcibiades if it could be possible to know the art of improving a ring, if one does not know what a ring is. Then in similar fashion he puts the question, 'and can we ever know what art makes a man better, if we do not know what we are ourselves?' He further asks, '..was he to be lightly esteemed, who inscribed the text on the temple at Delphi?' referring to the ancient Greek aphorism "Know Thyself" inscribed at the Temple of Apollo at Delphi. Socrates emphasised the importance of self-knowledge, which was carried further by his disciples such as Plato and Plato's student Aristotle.

Plato

Plato proposed a dualist theory, which states that that the soul is separate from the body. His tripartite theory of soul further elaborates on the nature of this entity. According to Plato, the soul is composed of three parts: the appetitive, the rational, and the spirited, (which in turn correspond to the three classes of a just society). Thus, it is made up of several elements with their own natural capacity and function:

Appetitive: This element refers to one's bodily appetites, desires, and needs. Certain forms of craving are needed for survival (e.g. hunger and thirst), and these exist alongside unnecessary appetitive cravings, such as the desire to over-indulge in food. This aspect of the soul loves pleasure, money and comfort. While temperance is the virtue that Plato associates with this element, its vices are lust and greed. In a society, the workers and merchants correspond to this part of the soul.

Rational: This part of the soul is concerned with differentiating the real from the apparent through the use of critical thinking. The ability to reason in order to live a good life comes from this aspect of soul. In fact, it is this ability to use language and reason which distinguishes humans from animals. This aspect of the soul is associated with the love of truth, wisdom and the act of analysis. Plato also suggests that the vices of pride and sloth could be associated with this element of the soul. The guardians of the republic or the 'philosopher kings' are the embodiment of the rational soul.

Spirited: this part of the soul is associated with desires for love, honor and victory. It is also associated with emotional drives such as anger, aggression, ambition, pride, loyalty and courage. When the desires of this spirited soul are not fulfilled, these negative emotions are felt. The function of this element of the soul is to ensure that the rational soul's commands are executed. The soldiers of a just society are the class associated with this aspect.

Aristotle

Aristotle's conception of the soul is quite different from that of his predecessors. A detailed description of this appears in his work *De Anima* meaning 'On the Soul'. For Aristotle there is no immortal soul that exists separately from the body. His conception arose from a rather unique postulation: that the soul can be defined as the very essential inseparable purpose of an entity. For example, the purpose of a knife is cutting. Now, the aspect of cutting cannot be separated from the knife, or the thing will no longer be a knife. Similarly, the primary activity of living is the essence of the soul. Such a soul or psyche has further secondary faculties such as nutrition, sensation, movement, reason etc.

Aristotle classifies souls in three hierarchical levels. At the bottom are plants, which exhibit functions of nutrition and reproduction; in the middle are the animals who, in addition to nutrition and reproduction, have sense perception and movement; at the top are humans who have all of these faculties, and the additional faculty of reason or intellect.

Rationalism

A distinct development of philosophy occurred in the West after the 16th century, building on the rationalist philosophy of

Descartes. Descartes' famous argument 'Cogito ergo sum' tries to eradicate doubt regarding whether the self exists. The existence of the very entity that doubts gets proven when such doubt arises; with this logic Descartes asserts the indisputability of the existence of the self. This led to the birth of the Enlightenment philosophy, the core of which was its understanding of the human subject. Descartes in particular could be said to have provided the foundations for this philosophical period. His philosophical method attacked the entire structure of earlier philosophy by questioning the proof of any so-called 'knowledge' that provided its basis. No assumption must be made, he argued, if its veracity cannot be proven. In his search for this proof, two arguments led Descartes to decide to begin at the beginning, so to speak; to distrust everything that he believed to simply be 'true.' The first of these arguments was that he could be dreaming: in a dream everything seems as real as it does whilst awake, so where is the proof that what one experiences is real or true? Indeed, how do we know that we are not continuously dreaming, and thus nothing is ever real? Descartes' second argument related to the concept of the 'evil genius': he questioned whether an external power could have created us, and could also have given us flawed cognitive facilities, thus ensuring that we will always have 'unreal' beliefs and experiences. Although he asserted the improbability of this, improbability for him was not a substitute for proof. He went on to philosophise therefore, that metaphysics must begin from truths which do not simply appear to be obvious, but which are self-confirming. In this regard he eventually produced his renowned statement *cogito ergo sum* (I think therefore I am), according to the following logic:

> I have convinced myself that there is absolutely nothing in the world, no sky, no earth, no minds, no bodies. Does it now follow that I, too, do not exist? No: if I convinced myself of something then I certainly existed. But there is a deceiver of supreme power and cunning who is deliberately and constantly deceiving me. In that case I too undoubtedly exist, if he is deceiving me; and let him deceive me as much as he can, he will never bring it about that I am nothing so long as I think that I am something. So after considering everything very thoroughly, I must finally conclude that this proposition, *I am, I exist*, is necessarily true whenever it is put forward by me or conceived in my mind. (Meditations. 2, AT 7:25).

The outcome of this line of thought was that the individual was conceptualised as fundamentally internal, rational and autonomous--entirely separate from physical processes which cannot so easily be proven real. Descartes could find no other aspect, apart from thought, which belonged to his 'essence.' For instance, although it seemed clear to him that he had a body, he could imagine himself existing as a thinking entity without that body (e.g. in heaven). This led directly to his suggestion that there is at least a possibility of immortality (Scruton, 2001).

Equally importantly, Descartes' form of rational thinking which led him to the 'truth' that the only definable part of man's essence is his thought, also ensured that thought (mind) became irretrievably separated from the material (body). According to

Grace Jantzen, Descartes' understanding of this duality directed him to determine that the 'thinking being defines itself by contrasting itself to all that can be considered not to think. The body and the material world become the non-thinking "Other" of the rational subject, to be brought under its strict control and mastery' (Jantzen, 1998. p. 32).

This led to the promotion of rationality as transcendent and disembodied. 'Thus, the equation of rationality and mind with truth was placed beyond doubt and the body was associated with a second-order, degraded ontology' (Hawthorne, 2006).

Starting from Descartes, what can be seen until today is a few centuries of development of thought in different phases, each advocating a certain philosophy, especially the philosophy of self.

Empiricism

As a critique of the rationalists, philosophy saw the emergence of empiricism, mainly marked by figures such as Hume and Locke. Their basic premise was that experiences hold the key to reality, and the self truly depends upon and gets created by each individual's bundle of experiences.

Locke

Empiricists such as John Locke (1632 – 1704) objected passionately to Descartes' assumption of an innate capacity for reason beyond experience, but they did not challenge his prioritisation of the self-sufficient subject. Locke's principal problem with Descartes' philosophy was the latter's insistence on a *pre-experiential* rational subject. Locke argued rather that the mind is a blank slate upon which ideas are created through sensory experience of the external world. He was challenged by other philosophers who remained loyal to Cartesian concepts, such as Leibnitz (1646 – 1716) , who insisted that the human being is born with innate ideas and innate knowledge. Spinoza (1632 – 1677) similarly suggested that the mind be visualised as a block of marble, veined in such a way that when knocked slightly with a hammer, it splits into a perfect figure of Hercules (in this sense, Leibnitz and Spinoza anticipated the 20th century Chomskyan concept of universal grammar). Thus while Locke tried to show that all ideas are dependent on experience, Leibnitz, Spinoza and others claimed that the content of certain ideas can be understood only through reason (and not experience), and consequently that there are certain a priori truths--a notion that Locke would not accept (Kramnick, 1995; Scruton, 2001).

Hume

Hume (1711 – 1776), too, was sceptical of any singular notion which regarded itself as holding the key to capturing the experience of 'self', a concept which he considered to represent the totality of one's life. Thus, there was no permanent soul in Hume's scheme of thinking. In his own words:

> For my part, when I enter most intimately into what I call *myself*, I always stumble on some particular perception or other, of heat or cold, light or shade, love or hatred, pain or pleasure. I never can catch *myself* at any time without a perception, and never can observe anything but the perception. (Hume, 1817. *Treatise*: 1.4.6.3).

Hume advocated a 'Bundle Theory' of self. The theory states

that what we call self is merely a collection of interconnected perceptions. These perceptions are often linked together because of perceived causal associations, coherences and consistencies. This gives rise to the *notion* of permanent self, whereas for Hume, self was nothing more than a bundle of experiences. He further criticised the glorification of the concept of independent self, which often resulted in the notion of an unchangeable permanent soul.

Idealism

Immanuel Kant (1724 - 1804) reconciled the opposing views of rationalist and empiricists with his famous theory of the pure universe of *noumena,* in which phenomena arise and disappear. He therefore brought a semblance of balance to these opposing theories and brought forth a theory that could define the self not in one, but two principles; the overriding primary principle of *noumena,* which establishes the essential existence of the self, and the concurrent assertion that phenomena or experiences shape this self. He noted that rationalists failed to give importance to this potential for shaping.

Kant attempted to bridge the gulf between empiricism and Cartesian rationalism by demonstrating that metaphysics must appeal simultaneously to both. In a gross simplification of his argument, Kant felt that empiricists, who prioritise experience above understanding, deny themselves access to the concepts through which experience may be understood. Likewise, he felt that pure rationalists, in their rejection of experience, 'deprive themselves of the very subject matter of knowledge' (Scruton, 2001). Kant's *Critique of Pure Reason*, published first in 1781, argues that before the person has any contact with the world and observes anything in it, there must be something there, an 'I' which can perceive. Every thought and sensory experience is channelled through this 'I.' Of course we do not preface every thought with 'I think,' but this is, Kant argues, inherent in the thinking process; this awareness of 'I think' sits quietly behind every thought. In short, every relationship that a person has with the world, however basic or intangible, is underpinned by the awareness of 'I':

> The 'I think' must be able to accompany all my representations; for otherwise something would be represented in me that could not be thought at all, which is as much as to say that the representation would either be impossible or else at least would be nothing to me. (Kant, 1781. Section 2:16).

In a sense therefore Kant's writing reflected Descartes' *cogito*; he insisted that prior to any interaction with the world, there must be an awareness of the self, and a sense of the self as a totality. This awareness is identified with thought: the self is thus the innate assumption of the stability and union of all of one's observations; it is the 'collection point of your thoughts' (Mansfield 2000). Kant's debt to Descartes is therefore his connection of the self with consciousness. His challenge to Descartes, on the other hand, rests in his assertion that the conscious 'I' is not the whole individual: it is the foundation of the subject, upon which the building blocks of experience are laid to make a coherent whole. In the quote just given, Kant makes clear that all experiences, all 'representations' or perceptions, must have a subject to whom they belong. All experiences or thoughts must be ascribable to a subject in order to justify being called an experience, thought or representation. Thus we cannot separate our understanding of (i.e. the meaning of) an experience from the perspective of the subject to whom the experience belongs (Atkins, 2000).

Phenomenology

Moving beyond empiricism, phenomenology emphasised the study of the structure of consciousness and the phenomena that appear in the consciousness. Husserl's views on the subject (ego) and the object are important in this regard.

Husserl

The phenomenon of sensory experience is central to a phenomenologist like Husserl (1859 - 1938). At the core of such knowing, we find the *Phenomenological Residue*. This residue is what remains after we remove transcendental and scientific data through abstraction and reduction. It exists in three forms: *ego, cogito,* and *cogitata.*

Phenomenological Ego: How do we know we exist? And what is the nature of such self or subject? Husserl gives the definition of a phenomenological ego, which is a stream of consciousness in which we get meaning and reality from our surrounding environment. And how do we become aware of such ego? For Husserl, it was the act of introspection that led to the phenomenological result creating human consciousness. By observing that we can touch and feel our being (even in the absence of any scientific proof), we know that we exist. Thus, such ego is always present and without it, nothing would exist.

Cogito: Various acts of consciousness, such as doubting, understanding, affirming, and denying, are called the cogitations or Cogito. These can be present only if there is self-awareness. Such cogitations give rise to the ego.

Cogitata: Consciousness is always a consciousness of something. There has to be an object of thought. Such objects are called cogitata. Husserl further points out that we cannot think about nothing, and nor can we deny nothing. The existence of a person or an individual depends on these *cogitata*. In absence of the object, there is no individual.

Husserl stated:

> Everything which is and has reality for me, that is, for man, exists only in my own consciousness. (Husserl, 1967. p. 31)

Thus, this phenomenological ego can understand itself through self-awareness of self-consciousness, the same way it learns about anything in its surrounding environment.

According to Husserl, through reduction the Phenomenological Ego can become an observer of itself, aware of itself, and self-conscious. Since we gain knowledge via this ego, we learn about the ego as we learn about the environment around us.

In his own words:

> We can describe the situation also on the following manner. If the Ego, as naturally immersed in the world, experiencingly and otherwise, is called 'interested' in the world, then the phenomenologically altered - and, as so altered, continually maintained--attitude consists in a *splitting of the Ego:* in that the

phenomenological Ego, establishes himself as 'disinterested onlooker', above the naively interested Ego. That this takes places is then itself accessible by means of a new reflection, which, as transcendental, likewise demands the very same attitude of looking on 'disinterestedly' - the Ego's sole remaining interest being to see and to describe adequately what he sees, purely as seen, as what is seen and seen in such and such a manner. (Husserl, 1967. p. 37)

Existentialism

Existentialism criticised the forms of philosophy popular at the time. This new philosophy emphasised the importance of the individual's feelings and very being. Existentialists saw a futility in the philosophies that tried to define the essence of the individual. For them, the existence came before the essence. Thus, the fact that we exist is of primary importance. Existentialism gives utmost importance to the struggle to find meaning in life, as well as the confusion and challenges of choice (which often lead to despair, angst, boredom, and anxiety).

The existentialist school produced numerous thinkers of significance, although it must be noted that these thinkers were by no means identical in their thought processes.

Kierkegaard

Kierkegaard is widely considered to be one of the pioneering existentialists. For him, abstract thinking held little importance. What was of primary importance was the individual subject. For

Kierkegaard, it was only through reflection and introspection that the individual became aware of the subjective self, not through scientific objective observation. The self held a very important place in his works, especially subjectivity. Subjectivity, he argued, always reflected itself by way of the choices, faith and commitment that the individual exhibits. For him, 'subjectivity is truth' and 'truth is subjectivity'. Thus the personal choices and the 'Leap of Faith' assume a great importance in one's life, according to Kierkegaard.

Kierkegaard was also a theologian and devout Christian. He believed that God established us and that He is part of our identity. For him our self-awareness happens reflexively and in choosing to be self-aware, we also become aware that we are aware of ourselves.

Kierkegaard further explained three spheres of existence. The aesthetic sphere is concerned with present happiness. The ethical sphere denotes a commitment to good actions and a religion that focuses on recognizing God as the one responsible for our lives, and the only one who give us the eternal happiness.

The same cannot be said about Nietzsche. For him, 'God was dead'.

Nietzsche:

Nietzsche was another major influence on existentialism. In the following quote, it is made clear that Nietzsche placed great importance on knowing oneself, and that he perceived a significant paradox in this.

> We are unknown to ourselves, we men of knowledge - and with good reason. We have never sought ourselves--how could it happen that we should ever *find* ourselves? ...there is

one thing alone we really care about from the heart -'bringing something home.' Whatever else there is in life, so-called, 'experiences'- which of us has sufficient earnestness for them? Or sufficient time? Present experience has, I am afraid, always found us 'absent-minded': we cannot give our hearts to it ....we sometimes ... ask, utterly surprised and disconcerted, 'what really was that which we have just experienced?' and moreover: 'who *are* we really? ...So we are necessarily strangers to ourselves, we do not comprehend our- selves, we *have* to misunderstand ourselves, for us the law 'Each is furthest from himself' applies to all eternity- -we are not 'men of knowledge' with respect to ourselves. (*Nietzsche*, 1968. p 451).

In the passage above, Nietzsche is pointing out that a significant part of ourselves is hidden from us. He believed that we are conscious of only a surface level of our psyche, and that the self is created by our experiences and actions. Unlike Kierkegaard, Nietzsche attributed the whole responsibility of one's actions to oneself. He gave a lot of importance to truth, and believed that truth is a feature of self. According to him, one must accept the truth of human existence, perhaps by 'suffering for truth's sake', even if it does not promise any pleasure to us.

Heidegger

Another stalwart in the existential camp was German philosopher Heidegger. He began a new era in philosophy by asking some fundamental questions that (as he rightly noted) philosophy ought to have asked, but never had. He claimed that since the time of Plato, philosophers were interested in discovering what "it" is that exists, resulting in the emergence of many theories that denote the qualities of such existing substance. For Heidegger, the still more fundamental question was, 'what does it mean to exist?' or 'what is it to exist?'. In their numerous attempts to describe the substance of existence, philosophers had failed to address the very nature of existence.

Earlier, Husserl's notion of 'intentionality' stated that there is no consciousness devoid of objects, meaning that consciousness is always directed towards something. Furthermore there is no object without consciousness holding it. Building on these concepts, Heidegger replaced all terms such as subject, object, consciousness and world with the German term *In-der-Welt-sein*, meaning Being-in-the-world.

A term also commonly used by Heidegger is *Dasein*, which has a similar meaning to the previous term. Although it is very hard to translate, if not impossible, it means "being-there" or "being-here". This was the new coinage of the term which he used to denote a 'human entity' that is 'already there' in the familiar world. The ability for language, intersubjective communication, and reasoning are associated with this *Dasein*.

The usage of such a concept was perhaps the very initial step towards understanding the most vital question raised by him: 'what is it to be?'. *Dasein* is not a result of philosophical analysis but something that we *are* in our day-to-day lives. Our very beings are *Dasein*. Thus, Heidegger's *Dasein* is different from the 'subject' that often is defined as consciousness or self. Heidegger wanted to avoid such descriptions and continued emphasise the use of the term *Dasein* to denote the very being of a human entity.

Heidegger defined the self of everyday - *Das Man* - as the 'they-self', which we distinguish from the authentic Self - - which is a being whose being is an issue for itself , or 'my owned self' as contrasted with 'the they self' or ' my un-owned self'.. As they-self, the particular Dasein disperses into the 'they', and must first find itself.

> If Dasein discovers the world in its own way [eigens] and brings it close, if it discloses to itself its own authentic Being, then this discovery of the 'world' and this disclosure of Dasein are always accomplished as a clearing-away of concealments and obscurities, as a breaking up of the disguises with which Dasein bars its own way." (Heidegger, 1962. p. 167).

Sartre

Sartre was amongst the most influential of the existentialist philosophers. Like other existentialists before him, he placed a great deal of importance on one's authentic experience of life, instead of knowledge. The following quote from his works highlights the importance he placed on choice, freedom and authenticity.

> If man, as the existentialist conceives him, is indefinable, it is because at first he is nothing. Only afterward will he be something, and he himself will have made what he will be. Thus there is no human nature, since there is no God to conceive it. Not only is man what

he conceives himself to be, but he is also only what he wills himself to be after this thrust toward existence. (Sartre, 1957. p. 13)

Antihumanism

What seems to be the common thread in the recent western philosophical schools of structuralism, analytical, post structuralism and post modernism is their spirit of anti-humanism, which rejects the existence of humans as autonomous subjects. These schools consider the study of human nature to be an out-dated metaphysical endeavour, better replaced by theories inspired by linguistics and anthropology.

Antihumanism suggests that humans are not autonomous and not individuals, but parts of society, thus advocating collectivism. Thinkers like Foucault (Foucault & Carrette, 1999, p. 6) attacked the notion of free will and consciousness, calling them sheer illusions.

In this way, western philosophy took another step from Nietzsche's assertion that "God is dead" to Foucault's "Man is dead".

Chapter 2

Self in Indian Philosophy

Whereas western thought in the area of self has developed most significantly in the last 500 years, questions related to self were addressed clearly in what are potentially the earliest records of Indian texts--the Vedas, which date back more than 3500 years. One of the four great sentences (*mahāvākyas*) of the Vedas is a response to the question: '*Koham?*' (Who am I?) which was answered by the revelations of the *rishis* as '*Soham*' or '*Tat tvam asi*', meaning 'Thou art That'[3] and '*Aham Brahmāsmi*', meaning 'I am Brahman',[4] declaring that the absolute Brahman, the essential eternal principal, is "That" who I am.

Indian philosophy comprises of several schools or *darśanas*. The *darśanas* are broadly divided into two groups: 1. The orthodox, or *āstika*, which consider the Vedas to be the ultimate philosophical authority and 2. The unorthodox, or *nāstika darśanas*.

---

3   Chāndogya Upaniṣad 6.8.7.
4   Bṛhadāraṇyaka Upaniṣad 1.4.10

There are six orthodox and three unorthodox schools. The following is the outline of the concept of self in each of these schools:

Sāṅkhya

Sāṅkhya can be termed one of the oldest Indian philosophical systems. It is a dualistic philosophy, in which there are two primary principles of *puruṣa* and *prakṛti*.

Puruṣa: Puruṣa is pure consciousness. It is above all--an indescribable, absolute and unknowable principle which is also the Transcendental Self. Thus *puruṣa* is the soul or the Self of all humans. Sāṅkhya acknowledges the plurality of *puruṣa*, which accounts for the existence of many selves or *jīvas* in the world.

Prakṛti: Prakṛti is the matter principle. The entire creation is caused because of *prakṛti* (except *puruṣa*). *Prakṛti* is devoid of any consciousness or intelligence. It gives rise to animate and inanimate beings. *Prakṛti* has three characteristics: *sattva, rajas* and *tamas. Sattva* is the principle of purity, order and balance. *Rajas* denotes activity and dynamism, whereas *tamas* literally meaning darkness, indicates inertia, dullness, lethargy. Through the combination and evolution of these three qualities, *prakṛti* creates the material world. The natural imbalance in these three qualities, or *triguṇas*, through twenty four principles, creates the evolution of *prakṛti*. This results in the world and nature, made of bodies and forms. These twenty four principles are:

Mahat: responsible for the rise of *buddhi or* discriminatory power (wisdom) in living beings.

Ahaṁkāra or ego-sense

Manas or '*Antaḥkarana*' (mind)

Pañca Tanmātrās or five objects (colour, sound, smell, taste, and touch)

Pañca jñāna indriyas or the five sense organs (eyes, ears, nose, tongue and body)

Pañca karma indriyas or the five organs of action (hands, legs, vocal apparatus, the urino-genital organ and the anus)

Pañca mahābhūtas or the five great substances – earth, water, fire, air and ether.

According to this philosophy, each individual simultaneously has *Puruṣa* as his/her essence, and his or her body and the physical environment are made of *prakṛti*. *Puruṣa* divides itself in multiple *jīvas* and then fuses itself with the products of *prakṛti* through the body, ego, intellect etc.

According to Sāṅkhya, ignorance about our true nature causes suffering, and the ability to differentiate between the dual principles leads to self-realisation, with ultimate freedom denoted by the state of *mokṣa*. Sāṅkhya is an atheist school and has no room for God in it.

Yoga

Very close to Sāṅkhya in its metaphysics, Yoga is often called the twin school of Sāṅkhya. While it builds upon the metaphysics of Sāṅkhya, Yoga differs from Sāṅkhya in its acceptance of the Godhead, making it a theistic school.

But what is truly distinct about Yoga is its detailed discourse on the dynamic path to enlightenment, or *mokṣa*. Yoga, primarily built around Patanjali's Yogasutra, provides a detailed path of practices that can finally lead to *kaivalya*--the union (literally, yoga) of the limited *jīva* with the limitless eternal.

The main practices of yoga are popularly known as *Aṣṭānga Yoga* i.e. the eight-fold path:

Yama: Abstentions

Ahiṁsā: abstention from violence

Satya: abstention from lying

Asteya: abstention from theft

Brahmacharya : abstention from sexual activity

Aparigraha : abstention from possessions

Niyama: Commitments to practice

Śaucha : purity

Santoṣa : contentment

Tapas : austerity

Svādhyāya : study

Īśvarapraṇidhāna : surrender to God

Āsana - Postures of the body

Prāṇāyāma - Control of *prana* or vital breath

Pratyāhāra – Abstraction or withdrawal of senses from the objects

Dhāraṇā – Concentration by focusing attention on a single object

Dhyāna - Meditation

Samādhi - Super-conscious state

Thus, one can see that Yoga lays a great deal of emphasis on the practices that would take one to the final destination of *kaivalya*. Patanjali's initial sutra stating 'Yogah chittavruttinirodhaha' underlines the philosophy of controlling the mental tendencies in order to awaken to the supreme self that one is, through practices such as meditation.

Nyāya

Nyāya is the school from which many schools of Indian philosophy drew influence for their systems of logic. Nyāya is essentially the system of logic, though not restricted to it. It also dwells on the issues of epistemology. Nyāya too is a dualist theory, and considers Self as eternal and the substratum of consciousness. Such self is devoid of actions and is not perceptible.

The Nyāya school was initially atheistic, but seemingly to differentiate itself from Buddhist thought, also atheistic, it developed a logical system to prove the existence of a single God.

In Nyāya, knowledge is the key to liberation, stating that self-knowledge and the right knowledge of the universe will free the individual from suffering, thus, it was the pursuit of knowledge which was advocated by the Nyāya school as a way to salvation.

Vaiśeṣika

The Vaiśeṣika school is based on Kaṇāda's theory that the universe is made of atom-like particles. Like Nyāya, it advocates a dualistic view of the universe. God is stated to be the force that infuses initial activity into these atoms. Owing to the similarities with Nyāya school, the two schools later merged.

Mīmāṃsā (or Pūrva Mīmāṃsā):

Apart from the metaphysical emphasis on knowledge, a major portion of the Vedas is devoted to various sacrificial fire rituals of *yajnas* and chanting of mantras. Mīmāṃsā or Pūrva Mīmāṃsā primarily focuses on this aspect of the Vedas and its interpretations. In that way it is basically hermeneutical in nature.

Unlike other schools, Mīmāṃsā is not focused on mokṣa or liberation by way of asceticism or mysticism. It opposes such ideas and strongly puts forth the view that it is by adhering to rituals in a disciplined way that one truly lives a life commanded by the Vedas. Thus, the entire emphasis of mīmāṃsā is on elucidating the importance of rituals and mantras. It also does not feel the need to infer the existence of Godhead. Its argument is that if the Vedas can be created without a creator, then so can existence as a whole. Overall, this approach upholds the unshakable authority of the Vedas, which is its primary purpose.

Vedānta or Uttara Mīmāṃsā

Vedānta (literally, Veda-end) is a school that focuses on the Upaniṣadic texts that appear at the end of the Vedas. The Upaniṣads are a group of texts that address fundamental spiritual questions pertaining to the deep meaning of existence, the self, Brahman and the paths for realisation of the ultimate truth. As opposed to pūrva mīmāṃsā, the Upaniṣads distance themselves from the rituals of *karmakāṇḍa*. The Upaniṣads have greater depth than any other Hindu texts—consequently, the philosophical enquiries carried out in the Upaniṣads have inspired many other spiritual traditions in Indian philosophy.

Owing to the fashion in which the Upaniṣadic texts are written, they leave room for various interpretations, subject to emphasis on different perspectives put forth in them. As a result, there are further subschools in the Vedānta school, as mentioned below:

Advaita: the non-dualistic school of Vedānta, is perhaps the one with the strongest and widest influence. Propagated by scholars such as Śaṅkaracharya, this school emphasizes that the whole existence is Brahman, which is eternal and omnipresent. It denies the existence of the world as real and calls it an illusion created by *Māyā*. Thus, it is a monist interpretation of the Upaniṣads. The path to realisation proposed by this school is *jñāna mārga* i. e. the path of knowledge. Upon removing the ignorance about the true nature of self and the universe, i.e. upon removing the *avidyā*, one permanently attains the ultimate state of *sat-cit-ānanda*, i.e. existence-consciousness-bliss, also known as *mokṣa*.

Viśiṣṭādvaita:

Viśiṣṭādvaita may be called qualified monism. Rāmānuja was the main proponent of this school, in which three primary elements are recognised: God, soul and the universe. Although all three are not separate and are in fact are manifestations of the same Brahman, Viśiṣṭādvaitins recognize their individual existence. Unlike the Advaita school, this school propagates the idea of *Saguṇa Brahma*, or Brahman with attributes. Viśiṣṭādvaita also recognizes the existence of individual souls. Although they are not separate from Brahman, they do have their individual existence. This also leads to the interpretation of this school as pantheistic.

The path of self-realisation in Viśiṣṭādvaita is that of *Bhakti* (devotion) and *Prapatti* (surrender). Viśiṣṭādvaita promotes Viṣṇu as God and prescribes surrender to his supremacy. *Māyā*, on the other hand, is seen as the creative power of God.

Dvaita

Madhvācārya, who led the Dvaita school, held some very strong and unconventional views, strongly opposing the Advaita schools. For dvaitins, Brahman referred to only one God – Viṣṇu. Matter and God were two separate principles – where Viṣṇu was the supreme God. The Dvaita school not only spoke about the difference between God and Matter, but it further asserted that each soul is separate from God, and each soul is separate from the other souls. Matter is different from the soul, and furthermore, all matter is not just tied to one principle – there are distinctions within matter too.

In a rather unconventional way, Dvaita argues for three different types of souls: those that will eventually get liberated (*Mukti-yogyas*), those that will remain in perpetual bondage (*nitya samsārins*), and finally those that will eventually be sent permanently to hell (*tamo yogyas*).

In summary, dvaitins reject the claim of advaitins that God and the self are one. They emphasise the supremacy of one single God - Viṣṇu - who is above everything.

Dwaitādvaita

Nimbārka proposed the philosophy of *Dvaitādvaita*. In this philosophy the individual soul or *jīva* is considered to be the same as Brahman, and yet from another perspective it can also be considered different from Brahman. Here too, existence is thought to consist of three principles: *Īśvara, cit*, and *acit*. Even though *cit* and *acit* are different from the *Īśvara*, they cannot exist without him, and thus they are solely dependent upon *Īśvara*, making them inseparable from him. It was primarily to highlight this separate yet totally dependent relationship between *cit – acit* and *Īśvara* that the philosophy of Dvaitādvaita was propagated.

Brahman here is Kṛṣṇa – the God above everyone. God plays a centrally important role in Dvaitādvaita philosophy, and surrendering to the God is the way to attain *mokṣa*. The school also gives four methods of practice that are helpful on the path to *mokṣa*. They are:

Karma – dutiful performance of rituals, *Vidyā* - knowledge, *Upāsanā* – meditations on God as the controller of *cit, acit* and as someone separate from these and finally *Gurupasatti* i.e. surrendering to one's Guru.

Śuddhādvaita

Śuddhādvaita, or purified non-dualism, was founded by Vallabhācārya and considers the individual soul to be the same as Brahma or Īśvara. It considers the individual soul to be part of the Īśvara, thus differing from the Advaita school. The individual soul has same properties of *sat-cit-ānanda* as that of Brahma or Īśvara, with the only difference being that the *ānanda* aspect, even though present, is not perceptible. Brahman is claimed to have divided itself into the 'many', and thus the universe is not merely *māyā* but Brahman itself.

Again, unlike Advaita philosophy, Śuddhādvaita prescribes *bhakti* to be the sole path towards liberation. According to Vallabhācārya, in the present time of *Kali Yuga, bhakti* is the only possible way to attain liberation. However, liberation 'Mukti' is not the highest ideal for which to strive. Instead of *Mukti*, it is the eternal service to Kṛṣṇa that is the ideal for Śuddhādvaita. Kṛṣṇa is considered the creator, and the creation is nothing but his *līlā*. One must totally surrender oneself (*ātmanivedana*): all of one's actions and the purpose of one's life are to unite with Kṛṣṇa alone. It is this *bhakti - puṣṭi bhakti* – along with the grace of God that is seen as the ideal way of life – this is not just the means, but the goal of life itself.

In summary, we see here the variety of positions advocated by different orthodox Indian schools. All of the philosophies adhere to certain views of the self, and depending on their metaphysical and ontological beliefs, a particular path to self-realisation is pre-scribed. The common thread among the orthodox schools is the faith they put in the authority of the Vedas. In no way do these schools refute or go beyond the word of the Vedas. Rather, it is only their unique ways of interpreting the Vedas that give the different characters to each school.

Below are the views of the non-orthodox schools, which differ significantly from those of the orthodox schools.

Cārvāka

In contrast to virtually all other schools of Indian philoso-phy, which promote striving to some sort of transcendental goal, Cārvākas teach that there is no reality beyond the material world. As such, they argue that one must not be fooled by different reli-gions, but rather focus on the sensory pleasures since there is no life after death.

Cārvākas criticised the Vedas and *pandits* and attacked the propagators of these beliefs as exploiters of society who made others believe in these things for their own selfish material interests. Thus, in Cārvāka we find a hedonist materialistic school of thought, which puts it at odds with every other school of Indian philosophy, whether orthodox or unorthodox.

Although a detailed discussion on the two other unorthodox schools – Jainism and Buddhism – will appear in the next chapters, they are briefly discussed in the following subsections.

Jainism

Having its roots in the ancient Indus valley civilization, Jainism may have been a spiritual tradition that grew in parallel to the Vedic religion. The primary focus of Jainism is the human being's effort to liberate himself/herself from the bondage of karma, towards liberation. The self, in its purest form, according to Jainism, is pure and infinite. However, due to being in the eternal world of birth and death, karma binds this pure soul to create bondage. This bondage leads to ignorance and suffering. The person with right faith, right knowledge and right character, with practices of meditation and *ahiṁsā*, attains *keval jnāna*.

There is no reference to the Vedas in Jainism, nor is there a concept of God. The emphasis is on one's effort to purify oneself. Every human is capable of attaining the highest status of a liberated siddha, if s/he makes the right effort towards liberation.

Buddhism

Similar to Jainism, Buddhism emphasizes individual efforts. One of the most radical and key principles of Buddhism is its notion of *anātma*--denial of the existence of a permanent self. According to Buddhism, everything is impermanent and therefore, there is no permanent self. This is a fundamental departure from most Indian schools. According to the Buddha (founder of Buddhism), self is perceived to be a permanent entity, owing to ignorance. Such ignorance can be removed by meditating upon the true nature of objects and perceiving the impermanence of everything. Such knowledge or realisation leads to freedom from birth and death and attainment of the blissful state of *nirvāṇa*, a state free from all suffering.

One can note that, other than the Cārvākas, all schools of Indian philosophy (whether orthodox or unorthodox) focus on the path to self-realisation in their teachings. These paths can be broadly classified in three categories: *Jñāna*, *Bhakti* and *Karma*.

The Three Paths

The paths of realizing the Truth or God or self (the self, which we will soon see, gets the status of 'the Self' with a capital S) seem to overlap with each other, owing to theories which put 'self-realisation' on an equal pedestal as realizing God, if not even higher than that. The three main paths found in the Indian tradition have been those of *Bhakti* (devotion) that of *Karma* (action), and finally the path of *Jñāna* (knowledge). The path of karma, due to its natural emphasis on actions or rituals, resulted in a different expression than that of *bhakti*, which placed great emphasis on faith and emotion. The proponents of each of these paths crafted a distinct lifestyle and attitude towards life and its various aspects. The path of karma created ritualists and *tāntrikas* whereas India's greatest saint poets claim a strong lineage in the path of *bhakti*.

However, it is the path of *jñāna* or knowledge that evolved and enriched the most significant part of what is known as Indian philosophy. These varied theories of self and self-realisation, which originated from some of the most influential thinkers of ancient and modern India, are the focus of this book.

Chapter 3

The Six Thinkers

India (traditionally known as Bharat) is a land rich in its exploration of human existence and the possibilities of the evolution of mind, body and soul. The advancement of culture in India dates back to several millennia BCE and the Vedic texts are definite examples of progress of human thought and language as early as about 1700 years BCE. The existence of several *darśanas* reflects the appreciation for diversity of opinions and richness of theories regarding human life and the existence of the universe.

The ocean of Indian philosophy is vast and deep. This book is focussed on the concept of self-realisation as stated by the key thinkers of ancient and modern India. Self-realisation often captures the most elevated of human possibilities, making manifest the essence of human existence and the climax of human evolution. Studying it, therefore, can provide a far greater understanding of the theory from which it emerges and also guide human endeavour towards the ideal which such a theory posits.

The selection of thinkers for this study is informed by period and by diversity of theory. From ancient India, Śaṅkarācarya of the Vedic tradition, Gautama Buddha of Buddhism and Mahāvīra of Jainism are studied. From modern India, Ramana Maharshi's path of self enquiry, Sri Aurobindo's integral yoga and J. Krishnamurti's approach of 'truth as a pathless land' are selected for research.

Śaṅkarācarya emphasized that Brahman (the Absolute) is the only reality, whereas this world is a false appearance, and the *jīva* or the individual soul is essentially not different from Brahman. Thus, he claimed that knowledge of this reality and freedom from *avidyā* as the path to enlightenment. The intellectual battle between Advaitins like Śaṅkarācarya and Buddhists has been historically popular. Where Śaṅkarācarya advocated the permanent Brahman, Buddhists denied existence of any permanent substance. The important Buddhist principles of *anātman* and *anitya* were opposed by Śaṅkarācarya. Mahāvīra on the other hand advocated the important principles of anekāntavāda and Syādvāda, taking a more balanced and relative view of reality. Mahāvīra's teachings that refer to karmic *pudgalas* resulting in bondage of the soul, and *nirjarā* as the path towards enlightenment, or *kevala jñāna,* was again heavily disputed by other contemporary schools of thought. These three views from ancient India form a core knowledge base that offers a rich diversity of views, leaving us compelled to take note of each one of them and critically analyse and synthesize each approach.

Modern India also saw some radical thinkers who influenced the world through their unique approaches towards self-realisation. Ramana Maharshi, whose teachings are considered to be very resonant with Advaita, essentially put forth the enquiry of 'who am I' as the main avenue to free one's consciousness of ego and to attain the state of pure consciousness, which, according to him, is the only reality.

Aurobindo had studied the Vedas but his theory and practice of Integral Yoga had uniquely different views than any historical or contemporary thinkers. He proposed that consciousness is One and is evolving. Man is not at the final end of the evolution. Thus, the next step in evolution is what he describes as the descend of the *Supermind* – a higher consciousness which will transform the human consciousness through the process of *supramentalisation*. Aurobindo wrote that whereas past teachings emphasized individual enlightenment as the final goal, his Integral Yoga considered enlightenment to be the first step, leading to freeing of the consciousness in matter. This evolved to the next level, in which the supramental replaces the mental and what he calls the super-man replaces the present man.

In the midst of such philosophies, J Krishnamurti took a radical stand against any method or theory or philosophy and showed that any method, process or system of thinking or belief will in fact keep the man in bondage. He believed that only choiceless awareness, which denies any past knowledge or conditioning, will free man. His teaching focussed on freeing man unconditionally from knowledge and past.

These three thinkers of modern India spoke a language that is more appealing to a population that, inspired by science and technology, regards logic as superior to faith or belief. The ancient views are popular with the more orthodox, who have a high regard for traditional scriptures. Due to the difference in metaphysical background of these theories and due to the unique language used by these thinkers, there is often a view that these philosophies are contradictory. However, there is a need to bring together these philosophies and analyse them. The attempt in this work is twofold: first, to arrive at a greater understanding of these approaches by in-depth and analytical study of each theory, and secondly, to arrive at a synthesis of understanding the human state and evolution to a possible state of self-realisation. Consequently, this work will guide individuals towards a holistic and integrated path of understanding and action in the domain of spiritual growth and self-realisation.

The synthesis primarily investigates questions like, is self-realisation as described by these different thinkers absolutely different? Or are there common elements? If there are differences, what are the metaphysical grounds on which these differences are based? Is it possible to hold a view that integrates these views on the state of self-realisation?

The synthesis will also focus on another important aspect, which is the process of self-realisation. As this work also includes the application of the theories discussed, it is important to see whether the different processes leading to self-realisation, as advocated by these thinkers, can be integrated. The synthesis of the processes investigates their similarities and differences. The findings are then critically analysed to understand the source and quality of differences, as well as the possibility of establishing some integrated processes which claim to bring about the state of self-realisation.

Finally, the synthesis covers the empirical aspects of self-realisation. It investigates whether there are categorical differences in experience of self-realisation according to different thinkers, or if there are certain elements which can be stated to essentially describe the experience of the process and state of self-realisation. This will focus on the affective, cognitive and behavioural aspects of the individual experience.

As indicated above, the self is studied at two levels: metaphysical and empirical. Although the metaphysical theories of different thinkers selected in this study are different, they can be explored if there is a synthesis of these approaches at metaphysical as well empirical levels. The question to address is whether it is possible to create synthesis at both, neither or only the empirical level? The question can also be further informed by critically looking into how the empirical and the metaphysical selves are related to each other.

Ancient Indian Thought on Self

Ādi Śaṅkarācārya
8th Century CE

What is enquiry into the Truth? It is the firm conviction that the Self is real, and that everything other than That is unreal.

Chapter 4

Ādi Śaṅkarācārya

BIOSKETCH

Born in south India, Śaṅkarā was an 8th century scholar, author and renunciate who criticised the ritualistic Vedic traditions to establish a monastic order and was the chief revivalist of the advaita vedanta philosophy. He travelled across the Indian subcontinent debating against Buddhism and other rival philosophies and thereby reigniting life into the main current of Hindu thought. Śaṅkarā is the main champion who re-established vedantic dominance in Indian philosophy, pushing against the tides of Buddhism and Jainism in India.

Śaṅkara was born circa 788 CE in south India. This was a time of ideological chaos in India. The dogmatic Brahminical philosophy had, over centuries, become ritualistic. Jain and Buddhist thought had made a significant impact by creating dents in the so-called Vedic Brahminical monopoly over truth and knowledge, which was widely popular in India. The decline in Vedic thought was largely a result of Brahminical ritualistic domination and the serious ideological challenges posed by strong philosophies of Jains and Buddhists. A few centuries after Buddha and Mahāvīra, there were declines in Jain and Buddhist ideologies as well, as a result of sectarianism and certain aspects of deterioration in religious practices. It is on this background that Śaṅkara, in a strong and definite way, created an impact by reviving the Vedic ideology and proposing his rather extreme theory of Advaita Vedānta.

Advaita Vedānta

The basic postulate of Śaṅkara's philosophy is that Brahman (the Absolute) is the only reality, whereas this world is non-real. The philosophy distinguishes between *asat* (unreal) and *mithyā* (which means neither real nor unreal). For example, dream objects and illusory objects are neither real nor unreal; they are different from 'unreal' objects such as the horn of a hare (which does not exist). The world is compared to illusory objects. Like them, the world appears to us and hence it cannot be called absolutely unreal. Rather, it gets sublated or vitiated due to realisation of Brahman. Hence, the world cannot be called absolutely real either. Thus, it falls in the category of neither real nor unreal, which is the same as *mithyā*. Thus, the jīva or the individual soul is essentially not different from Brahman. Śaṅkara argues this in the following comment on one of the *sūtras* of *Brahma sūtras*. He backs his claim by giving references from various Upaniṣads.

> According to the *Śrutis*, the Jīva is eternal,
> birthless and changeless. It is the unchanging

Brahman itself that exists as the Self. Which are those *Śrutis*? "The individual self does not die" (Chāndogya Upaniṣad 6-11-3) "That Self is without any decay, immortal, fearless and Brahman" (Bṛhadāraṇyaka Upaniṣad 4-4-25) The intelligent one is not born and does not die; This ancient one is birthless, eternal and unchanging (Kaṭhopaniṣad 1-2-18). "Having created that, He entered into that (Taittīriya Upaniṣad 2-6-1) "Let me manifest myself as name and form entering as the individual self" (Chāndogya Upaniṣad 6-3-2). "This Self permeates those bodies up to the tips and nails (Br.1-4-7) "Thou art That " (Chāndogya Upaniṣad 6-8-7) "I am Brahman " (Br,1-4-10) "This Self , the perceiver of everything, is Brahman" (Bṛhadāraṇyaka Upaniṣad 2-5-19) These and other *Śrutis* speak of eternality deny the origin of the individual Self. (Brahmasūtra Śaṅkarabhāṣya 2-3-11-17)

Thus, knowledge of this reality and freedom from *Avidyā* was claimed by him as the path to self-realisation.

In order to assert the highest absolute principle – the Brahman – stated in Upaniṣads – and to establish its supremacy, Śaṅkara gave it the status of something which is eternal i.e. without beginning or end, non changeable and omnipresent.

It is without parts, without action, changeless, defectless and without virtue or vice. It is the supreme bridge to immortality. It is like the fire which has burnt its fuel. (Śvetāśvatara Upaniṣad 6-19).

The normal experience of humans is far from this. Everyday experience is full of perishable things, transient and subject to death and destruction. Once a theory grants existence to these finite forms, it has to explain their origin and their relationship with the so called eternal absolute principle. Then arise the questions of supremacy and the possible dependence or independence of these two aspects of reality. Giving a status of reality to material things would have created serious challenges to Śaṅkara's theory, eventually pushing him to attribute some limitations to the principle of Brahman (for which it seems he wasn't ready). In fact, it would have shaken the very foundation of Śaṅkara's theory, which as he claimed was based on his famous interpretations of the major Upaniṣads and Bhagavadgītā. In reality, these original texts seldom took this massive stance of attributing the sole status of reality to Brahman.

Māyāvāda

In order to explain the experience of mortality of life and things, the attribute that has no room in the magnificent splendid Brahman, Śaṅkara proposed that all experiences, in phenomenological terms, are like illusions and do not have absolute reality.

In his commentary on the Brahma *sūtras*, after briefly discussing the nature of the world, Śaṅkara denies the reality of creation and calls it a delusion, or *māyā*. His logic is that, according to Vedas, cause and effect are not different, and hence Brahma is the sole reality; how can the world (the effect) be any different?

Thus, the apparent transitory world must be non-existent – or just a false appearance.

> And yet the creation of space etc. also has no absolute reality; for under the aphorism "the effect is non-different from the cause since terms like 'origin' etc are met with, we showed that the whole creation is but Māyā. (Brahmasūtra Śaṅkarabhāṣya: 3-2-4)

One can then ask the pertinent question, "does *Māyā* exist?". Again we have to answer in the negative, as per Śaṅkara's theory that nothing impermanent exists except for Brahman. The Māyāvāda provides a detailed explanation of how illusion is based on reality, but appears to exist only until reality is seen, as in the famous example of a rope being perceived as a snake.

If we deny the existence of any form, it leads to an end of the dialogue, as any discussion or description invariably falls into the realm of non existing *māyā*. This makes it impossible for mind (if any such thing exists at all) to speak about Brahman, since by definition, Brahman is indescribable.

> Thus the knowledge of Brahman is not dependent on human action. What then? It is on the thing itself, like the knowledge of a thing got through the valid means, such as direct perception etc. It is impossible to imagine such a Brahman or its knowledge to be gained by any logic. Nor it is possible to understand the work of Brahman by virtue of its being the object of the act of knowing. As from the *Śrutis*, "It is

different from the known and also different from the unknown" (Kenopnishad, 1.4), "Through what one should know That by which all this is known." (Bṛhadāraṇyaka Upaniṣad, 2-4-14), the object of the act of knowing is denied. Similarly, the object of the action of meditation is also denied. The *Śruti* "That which is not revealed by speech , by which speech is revealed" after declaring that Brahman is not an object, says "Know that alone as Brahman and not what people meditate on."(Kenopnishad, 1-1) (Brahmasūtra Śaṅkarabhāṣya,1-1-4-4)

Such a drastic stance has a unique impact. Such a strong monistic idealistic theory creates a simple yet strong emphasis on certain ideology, bypassing the hassle of explaining the so-called stark realities of everyday mundane life and its challenges, and eventually establishing a particular supreme ideal, in this case Brahman. Historically, when Śaṅkara's theory emerged in the chaos of Indian ideological clashes and deterioration of the prevailing Hindu beliefs, it made a massive impact and strongly established itself. Furthermore, it revived certain socio-religious sections of society and created new ideals and new structures, the details of which (like the *varna* and caste system) will not be engaged with here, as they clearly lie outside the scope of this book.

Self

The subconscious quest of humans for permanence and immortality has been evident across the centuries. Posed with the challenge of death and decay of both self and material possessions, humans have always sought something that is beyond limitations. The popularity of the idea of God as a supreme omnipotent force could be attributed to this quest of humans. In the words of J. Krishnamurti, it is not God who created humans, but humans who have created God. Śaṅkara equated self and Brahman. His theory does away with the concept of God and replaces it with Brahman, which has no attribute. This takes away the duality of the God and the seeker. In fact the very self or *Jīva* / atman is Brahman. Śaṅkara, as mentioned in the last chapter, was keen to show that his theory was based on knowledge of the Upaniṣads. The Upaniṣads, a scattered body of verses, are far from being consistent in their philosophical assertions, giving rise to a variety of interpretations. Śaṅkara, in his commentaries on specific Upaniṣads, ultimately did find enough ground to support his ideology. In his collection of verses on self-realisation titled *Aparokṣānubhuti* (direct experience), he references the Bṛhadāraṇyaka Upaniṣad 2.5.19, quoting the *Śruti* asserting *Ātman* as Brahman. The Upaniṣad says:

'This Brahman has no antecedent or consequent, no interior or exterior. This self, the all-perceiving, is Brahman. This is the teaching of the Upaniṣads.'

Śaṅkara had a great affinity for the Upaniṣads, but was equally comfortable discarding almost all the rituals of earlier Vedic texts. He proclaimed that the rituals had little or no significance in life, and at least in his writings and teachings, they did not.

Self-realisation

At several places in his writings Śaṅkara reiterates the supremacy of the path of Knowledge. The understanding, recognition and realisation of Brahman are the sole important accomplishments in life.

Śaṅkara's commentary on the legendary Bhagavadgītā is one of his most revered works.The Gītā primarily speaks of Jñāna, Bhakti and Karma as paths towards self-realisation. Śaṅkara's interprets it differently though. For Śaṅkara, jñāna is the only path. It is only by the knowledge of (these) principles, that the liberation is possible, not by various actions (*rituals*) like rites and duties. This is the definite interpretation. (Gītābhāṣya 18.46).

Thus, the definite conclusion in the Gītā is that Liberation is attained only from the knowledge of Reality, and not from its combination with action (Gītābhāṣya 18.50). And by pointing out in Gītābhāṣya (2.21) that "there could be no rescue other than through the knowledge of the Self", and from the statement that action is impossible for man of realisation, it is understood that the conclusion of the Lord is that, actions enjoined by the scriptures are prescribed for the unenlightened.

Śaṅkara clarifies that "Seekers of liberation are qualified only for renunciation of all rites and duties. Indeed, even the Lord Nārāyaṇa makes a distinction between the enlightened man of Knowledge and the unenlightened man who performs rites and duties" (Gītābhāṣya 18:66)

Has knowledge been established as the supreme means to Liberation in the Gītā, or is it action? Or both? Why does this doubt arise? (Because) passages such as, '...by realizing which, one attains Immortality' (Gītābhāṣya 13.12), and 'Then, having known Me in truth, he enters (into Me) immediately after that (Knowledge)'. point to the attainment of Liberation through Knowledge alone.

Śaṅkara again refutes the rival position by stating "the highest good cannot be attained through mere actions, nor by a combination of Knowledge and action." This he further backed by quoting the Upaniṣads: 'Knowing Him alone, one goes beyond death; there is no other way to go by' (<u>Śvetāśvatara</u> Upaniṣad 3.8), illuminating that for Liberation there is no other path but enlightenment. Also supporting this is the Upanisadic statement that Liberation for an unenlightened person is as impossible as the rolling up of the sky like leather (<u>Śvetāśvatara</u> Upaniṣad 6.20)

This is also confirmed in his commentary on the Brahmasūtras (3-4-1-1): "The Śruti speaks of knowledge alone as the cause of liberation."

Although at a pure ideological level, any prescription of any path to self realisation creates challenges which might be difficult to answer by strictly adhering to Śaṅkara's theory. This is because the self, as normally experienced by humans, does not exist at all in Advaita ideology. So who will realise Brahman? Brahman alone can realise Brahman and apparently without effort or path! Yet, a philosophy so idealistic will not appeal to the layman, and so it may not achieve the purpose it sets out to achieve. This gave rise to what was elaborated by Śaṅkara as the concept of *Prātibhāṣika Sattā*, the apparent reality.

Śaṅkara uses popular ideological terms of that time to have a discourse on several elements that were constituted as elements pertaining to self. These were the trigunas, the *manas, buddhi, citta, ahaṅkāra*, the body etc. Śaṅkara would refer to each but eventually deny their existence, as Brahman alone exists.

So what did he recommend as the path of realisation?

The place of Rājayoga and Haṭha Yoga

As guidance for steps to achieve self-realisation, Śaṅkara uses the key concepts from Patanjali's Yoga Sutra which were laid out almost a thousand years before his time as part of the Sāṅkhya *darśana*. However, he gives an advaitic flavour to this. In Aparokṣānubhūti, verses 100 to 125 Śaṅkara describe the fifteen steps to attain self-realisation. He uses practically the same terms as those that appeared in the eight-step Aṣṭānga Yoga model of Patanjali. He starts with *yama, niyama* and goes on till *dhyāna* and *Samādhi*. The difference here is that each step, including the breathing exercise *prāṇāyāma* and *āsanas* (postures), are tied to Brahman. Thus, in Śaṅkara's philosophy, the meaning of each of Patanjali's sutras is altered. The five aspects of good conduct i.e. *Yama (Ahiṁsā, Satya, Asteya, Bramhacarya,* and *Aparigraha)* are replaced with restraint of all senses, with the knowledge that "all this is Brahman". Naturally, when the world does not have absolute existence, Śaṅkara does not dwell much upon virtues such as non-killing-- as the perishable doesn't really exist, and that which really exists is immortal. Śaṅkara warns the seekers that there is no use in practising difficult yogic postures and concentrations, as the only posture that is useful is the one in which there is spontaneous meditation of Brahman. Instead of practising *trāṭaka* (concentrating your vision on an object) the noblest vision is that which sees the world as Brahman. The following verse (116 & 117) from his book Aparokṣānubhūti exemplifies this:

> By converting one's vision into that of knowledge, one must realise the whole world as Brahman itself. This is the most useful vision, not that which is focused on the tip on the nose.

In this verse he further illustrates that various yogic techniques (like concentration and *trāṭaka*) are inadequate for realising the truth:

> Or, the vision should be directed solely upon that in which the distinction between the seer, seen and seeing ceases. It need not be directed to the tip of the nose.

Clearly for Śaṅkara, only that which takes one's awareness to Brahman qualifies as a worthwhile attempt.

Śaṅkara repeatedly denounces any importance of karma, *prārabdha* (the accumulated past *karmas*) and its result in form of cycle of birth and death (a concept that was, as we will see in next section, central to Buddhist and Jain philosophies). Even if the concept of *prārabdha* appears in *Śrutis*, which Śaṅkara considers as authority. His theory is based on *Śrutis*, and he often warns that not believing in them will be sinful and disrespectful. However, he finds a way to explain his deviations from the theory by adding that concepts like *prārabdha*, even if mentioned in *Śrutis*, are only for the ignorant. After describing the Brahman oriented yogic practices, he once again reminds his audience that *Rāja-yoga* i.e. the meditation and realisation that the self and the world is Brahman alone is the supreme path, is alone sufficient for advanced seekers. For those less evolved, they can additionally practice *Haṭha yoga*. He does makes a passing reference to the intermediate usefulness of devotion to teacher and deity as an aid in purifying the mind, which is then benefited by *Rāja-yoga* in perfecting self-realisation.

Buddha
5th Century BCE

"It is better to conquer yourself than to win a thousand battles. Then the victory is yours. It cannot be taken from you."

Chapter 5

Buddha

BIOSKETCH

Born in the 5th century BCE in East India, Buddha was the enlightened preacher who established the monastic tradition where monks (and later nuns) practiced a renunciate but 'middle path' of meditation to enlightenment. Buddha preached mostly in eastern India and his followers spread the teachings to the Far East and South-East Asia. Today, his teachings have directly and indirectly influenced various branches of Buddhism, which is the world's 4th largest religion with more than 500 million followers, predominantly in Asia.

Siddhārtha Gautama (563 BCE to 483 BCE) later known as Gautama, the Buddha or just Buddha perhaps was not the first of his kind. The *Śramaṇa* tradition has been active and alive in India since prehistoric times. There have been records that point to the possibility that *Śramaṇa* tradition might be much older than the Brahmnical traditions of India. *Śramaṇa* traditions were basically non-Vedic, inspired by several enlightened or liberated persons and their teachings which were unorthodox and required people to work for their own salvation – hence the name, *Śramaṇa* (lit. work-out).

Buddha could be named as perhaps the most popular teacher of this tradition. He largely worked on his own in search of the truth, found his own answers and shared this original understanding with people who were interested in it. Unlike Śaṅkara, Buddha was more of a teacher than a philosopher. But soon a philosophy was to form around his teaching, leading to several interpretations, as is common with most popular ideologies. In this book I have primarily relied on the original texts, and avoided the details of the debates amongst different schools which broke away from the main teachings. The Tipiṭakas are the commonly agreed to be the most authentic and oldest accounts of Buddha's teachings. The discussion in this book is based on the core concepts relevant to the subject matter that is discussed in these canonical texts.

The noble truths

The essence of Buddha's teaching is captured in the four noble truths. It is believed that Buddha taught these in his very first discourse after his enlightenment. The description of these truths appears in *Dharmacakra-Pravartana-Sūtra*, the discourse that set the wheel of *dharma* rolling. The following text is the translation of Buddha's words from his very first discourse after the enlightenment.

> There are these Four Noble Truths, monks.
> Which four? Suffering, the arising of suffering,

the ending of suffering, and the practice leading to the ending of suffering.

What is suffering? Birth is suffering, old age is suffering, sickness is suffering, death, being connected to what is not dear, being separated from what is dear, is suffering. Not to get what one seeks for is suffering. In brief, the five constituent parts (of mind and body) that provide fuel for attachment are suffering. This is suffering.

What is the arising of suffering? It is that craving which leads to continuation of existence, which is linked with enjoyment and passion. This is the arising of suffering.

What is the ending of suffering? It is the complete fading away and ending without remainder of the birth of that craving, which greatly enjoys this and that, and is linked with enjoyment and passion. This is the ending of suffering.

What is the practice leading to the ending of suffering? It is the noble eightfold path, which is: right view, right thought, right speech, right action, right livelihood, right endeavour, right mindfulness and right concentration. This is said to be the noble truth of the practice leading to the ending of suffering.

These, monks, are the four noble truths. (Saṃyutta Nikāya, 56:11)

Interestingly, whereas the Upaniṣadic, Vedic Brahman is *ānanda* – the blissful, Buddha's first noble truth is about Sorrow. To summarise, the four truths are: 1. *Duḥkha*: that there is suffering (that of birth, old age, disease and finally death) 2. *Tṛṣṇā*: the reason of sorrow is desire or craving 3. *Nirvāṇa*: there is end of all sorrow 4. *Dharma*: there is a way to attain *nirvāṇa*. The question that we will focus on presently, is whose *nirvāṇa*? What is a person according to Buddha?

The Three marks of existence

In the Buddha's teachings there are three characteristics shared by all conditional things, namely: impermanence (anitya), suffering or unsatisfactoriness (*duḥkha*), and non-self (*anātman*).

Impermanence (*Anitya*): Buddha said,

> "The five aggregates, monks, are *anitya*, (impermanenence). All is impermanent. And what is the all that is impermanent? The eye is impermanent, visual objects (*Rūpa*)... eye-consciousness... eye contact (*cakku-samphassa*)... whatever is felt (*vedayita*) as pleasant or unpleasant or neither-unpleasant-nor-pleasant, born of eye-contact is impermanent. [Similarly, with the ear, nose, tongue, body, and mind] (Samyutta Nikaya: 35.43)

> All formations are impermanent. Whatever is subject to origination (*samudaya*) is subject to cessation (*nirodha*)." (Majjhima Nikaya 56)

Dissatisfaction (*Duḥkha*): *Duḥkha*, commonly translated as suffering, has a deeper meaning than just pain or unpleasant suffering. It means the pervading sense of dissatisfaction with everything in life. Although Buddha acknowledges the existence of happiness, he says that the impermanent nature of being leaves us with a feeling of overall dissatisfaction. The main sufferings according to Buddha are those related to the uncomfortable experience of birth, aging and old age, disease and death. Suffering also includes the sorrow of not getting what we want and being subjected to that which we do not want. And finally, it includes the all-pervasive dissatisfaction owed to the impermanence of everything.

Non-self (*anātman*): While explaining the non-self principle, Buddha stated (Majjhima Nikaya 3.196):

> "...form is not the self (*anātman*), sensations are not the self, perceptions are not the self, assemblages are not the self, consciousness is not the self. Seeing in this way, this is the end of birth, the Brahman life has been fulfilled, what must be done has been done."

In the Dharmapada (20, 277 – 279), we find all the three principles of *Anitya, Duḥkha* and *Anātman* asserted: 'All processes are impermanent ... All processes are afflicted ... All phenomena are not 'Self'; when this is seen with knowledge, one is freed from the illusion of affliction. This is the pathway to purity.'

Thus, one can note the contrast that the Buddha denied the very thing that the Upaniṣads asserted. For Buddha, there is nothing permanent, and thus, there is no permanent self or soul. What we have is faulty perception of a permanent self, whereas what is real is that everything is constantly changing. If we say that the self is changing, then that would not be true, for there needs to be assumption that there is a constant self which is undergoing changes. For Buddha, everything is always changing, and there is nothing as a permanent self. Then what is self? It is merely an appearance put up together by the *sanghata* of various elements that come together. When we try to understand what a chariot is by systematically examining it, we will only find parts, and no chariot. Similarly, what we call a self is an illusion that comes into existence as different elements bound together. This negation of self is central to Buddha's teachings because it is the 'I' that becomes the centre of all cravings and aversions – the very root of sorrow. When there is a clear perception of *anitya* or impermanence, naturally the craving ceases and one enters *nirvāṇa* – the final goal – that promises the end of the cycle of birth and death – a goal very similar to the Vedantic goal of *Mokṣa*. While in *nirvāṇa* there is complete annihilation and cessation, in mokṣa, there is complete identification with the permanent Brahman. Both goals promise freedom from burdens of mortality and its sorrows, by removing the *avidyā*, but in *nirvāṇa* you cease to exist and in *mokṣa* you exist permanently.

Ārya Aṣṭāngika Mārga

Buddha carved the path of *nirvāṇa* in a systematic way. Compared to Śaṅkara, one can observe here much more attention given to the step-by-step progress of the aspirant. The three gems of Buddhism guide an aspirant on this path: the Buddha, the *dharma* and the *sangha*. The *dharma* – the teachings – are well elaborated in an eight step model. In the Saṁyukta Nikāya, sutra 287, Buddha summarises the noble path as follows:

> In the same way I saw an ancient path, an

ancient road, travelled by the Rightly self-awakened ones of past times. And what is that ancient path, that ancient road, travelled by the Rightly self-awakened ones of past times? Just this noble eightfold path: right view, right aspiration, right speech, right action, right livelihood, right effort, right mindfulness, right concentration.. I followed that path. Following it, I came to direct knowledge of aging & death, direct knowledge of the cause of aging & death, direct knowledge of the ending of aging & death, direct knowledge of the path leading to the ending of aging & death...Knowing that directly, I have revealed it to monks, nuns, male lay followers & female lay followers...

These eight steps broadly fall into one of the following three categories:

Wisdom (prajñā)

> Right understanding
> Right Intention

Ethical conduct (Śila)

> Right speech
> Right action
> Right livelihood

Meditation (Samādhi)

> Right effort
> Right mindfulness
> Right meditation

One can see here a keen focus on the individual. There is no god in Buddhism (as reflected in teachings of Buddha), no idol to worship, but the only ideal of nirvāṇa, which is common to all and equally attainable by all. The *saṅgha* was designed to keep the serious seekers together and Buddha took great care in chalking out the rules for this *saṅgha,* as later compiled by monks in the *Vinaya Piṭaka*. For monks and nuns or for lay people, the key aspects of Buddha's path for realisation are clear: moral conduct as a basic foundation and the most important practice of meditation (in which the *tṛṣṇā* is seen closely and clearly, and impermanence is fully captured). This finally leads to the awakening of *prajñā* (wisdom) as *anitya* (impermanence) thereby opening the doors of *nirvāṇa*. The steps of these meditations are elaborated as:

The *Dhyānas*

The description appears as stated by Buddha in the <u>Anuppada Sutta,</u> (Majjhima Nikaya 111).

The *Rūpa Dhyānas*

There are four stages of deep collectedness which are called the *Rūpa Dhyāna* (Fine-material *Dhyāna*):

First *Dhyāna* - 'directed thought, evaluation, rapture and pleasure'

Second *Dhyāna* - 'internal assurance, rapture, & pleasure'

Third *Dhyāna* - 'equanimity-pleasure'

Fourth *Dhyāna* - 'a feeling of equanimity, neither pleasure nor pain; and an unconcern due to serenity of awareness'.

The *Arūpa Dhyānas*

After the four *dhyānas* come four attainments. Also known as the formless *dhyānas* (*arūpadhyānas*), or The Formless Dimensions:

Dimension of Infinite Space - perception of the dimension of the infinitude of space.

Dimension of Infinite Consciousness - perception of the dimension of the infinitude of consciousness.

Dimension of Nothingness - perception of the dimension of nothingness.

Dimension of Neither Perception nor Non-Perception - About the role of this *dhyāna* in Buddha's own experience, it is said: 'He emerged mindfully from that attainment. On emerging mindfully from that attainment, he regarded the past qualities that had ceased & changed: 'So this is how these qualities, not having been, come into play. Having been, they vanish.' He remained unattracted & unrepelled with regard to those qualities, independent, detached, released, dissociated, with an awareness rid of barriers. He discerned that 'There is a further escape,' and pursuing it, he confirmed that 'There is.'

The mental factors of unification of mind, contact, feeling, perception, intention, consciousness, desire, decision, persistence, mindfulness, equanimity and attention are common to all *dhyānas*.

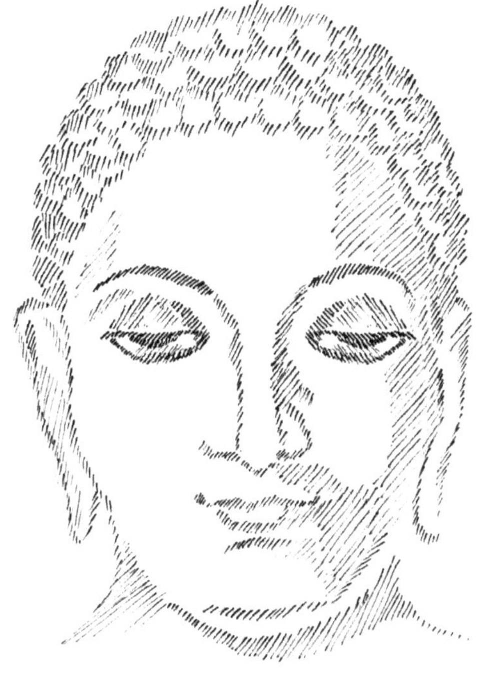

Mahāvīra
5th Century BCE

When you discover for yourself, however dimly,
that you are rooted in something that is infinitely
vast and potential, you have found the soil wherein
you grow into a most wonderful tree, the tree of life
blended with knowledge

Chapter 6

Mahāvīra

BIOSKETCH

A lesser known contemporary of Buddha, Mahāvīra, was the 24th Tīrthaṅkara of the ascetic Śramaṇa tradition which focused solely on the path of nonviolence, meditation and renunciation to achieve victory over ignorance. Mahāvīra was the first proponent of nonviolence, which contradicted both the prevalent violent Vedic rituals, as well as the pursuit of a materialistic life. Mahāvīra was born in 5th century BCE in east India, whence his influence spread across the India subcontinent. Various prominent kings and scholars adopted Jainism – the way of life as taught by him. Today, 4 to 5 million people belong to the Jain religion.

With regard to the background of the soul-asserting and soul-denying theories of Śaṅkara's Advaita Vedānta and Buddhism respectively, there existed another prominent and influential school, relatively less studied, but perhaps unique and extraordinary in its logic and impact. It is, nevertheless, one which cannot be ignored when we talk about self-realisation in ancient India. This is the Jaina school of thought known as Jain *darśana* or Jainism.

Jainism, like Buddhism, belongs to the śramaṇa traditions of India. The first personality of this school, widely known as Ādinātha R̲ṣabhadeva, appears in various texts of the Vedas and many *purāṇas*, such as Bhāgavata, etc. It is difficult to estimate the period in which R̲ṣabhadeva flourished, although there is consensus among a number of researchers that the excavations related to the Indus Valley Civilization show a strong link to R̲ṣabhadeva. The period of R̲ṣabhadeva can be roughly estimated as being at the end of Stone Age or the beginning of the agricultural age. He is also considered as being the founder of the *Śramaṇa* tradition.

An important and enlightened teacher, who contributes to establishing 'bridges' to the 'other shore', is called a *Tīrthaṅkara*. Jain texts claim that each time cycle contains 24 *Tīrthaṅkaras*. R̲ṣabhadeva was the first one. Historians have been able to find references to the 23rd *Tīrthaṅkara*, Parśvanātha, whose teachings were further revised in terms of their relevance for the contemporary age by the 24th and last *Tīrthaṅkara*, Vardhamāna Mahāvīra.

Mahāvīra lived from 599–527 BCE. His teachings are captured in the *āgmas*, viz, Ācāranga sūtra, Sūtrakrtanga, etc. What is studied as Jainism today derives from Mahāvīra's teachings as its primary source.

The seven principles:

Jīva

Jainism believes that souls (*jīva*) exist as reality. *Jīva* is characterized by *chetana* (consciousness) and *upayoga* (knowledge and perception). The soul is eternal, neither born nor subject to death.

Ajīva

Ajīva are the five non-living substances that make up the universe along with the jīva. They lack consciousness. They are:

Pudgala (Matter)

Matter is classified as solid, liquid and gaseous energy. It also includes the Karmic materials, a concept unique to Jainas. *Pudgalas* too are permanent and indestructible. They can be combined or they may change modes, but they too are granted eternal status.

Dharma-tattva (Medium of Motion) and *Adharma-tattva* (Medium of rest)

They are also known as *Dharmāstikāya and Adharmāstikāya*. *Dharma-tattva* and *adharma-tattva* mediate motion and rest in other bodies.

Ākāśa (Space)

Space is a substance that accommodates souls, matter, the principle of motion, the principle of rest, and time. It is all-pervading, infinite and made up of infinite space-points.

Kāla (Time)

Time is a real entity according to Jainism, and all activities, changes or modifications can be achieved only through time.

Āsrava

The *āsrava* is the influx of karmas. It occurs when the karmic particles are attracted to the soul on account of vibrations created by activities of mind, speech and body.

Bandha

The karmas have effect only when they are bound to the consciousness. This binding of the karma to the consciousness is called *bandha*. *Pāpa* and *Punya* are two types of *bandhas*, meaning demerit and merit respectively.

Saṃvara

Saṃvara is stoppage of karma. The first step to emancipation or the realisation of the self is to see that all channels through which karma has been flowing into the soul have been stopped, so that no additional karma can accumulate. This is referred to as the stoppage of the inflow of karma (saṃvara).

Nirjarā

Nirjarā is the shedding or destruction of karmas that have already been accumulated. Nirjarā is of two types: the psychic aspect of the removal of karma (*bhāva-nirjarā*), and destruction of the particles of karma (*dravya-nirjarā*).

Mokṣa

Mokṣa means liberation, salvation or emancipation of the soul. It is a blissful state of existence of a soul, completely free from the karmic bondage, free from *samsara*, the cycle of birth and death. (Glasenapp, 1999)

Self and self-realisation

Thus, one can see that every soul or jīva is, in a way, individual. This results in Jain philosophy being classified as pluralist. Of course, whether it is monist, dualist or pluralist will have to be examined within the framework of Anekāntavāda and Syādvāda. Mahāvīra's is definitely not a monistic theory, for there is a distinct assertion of two principles, viz., life and matter.

Individuality comes into existence on account of several *pudgalas* which cling to the soul, the soul which, in principle, is infinite. The way in which this self realises its ideal state is the path highlighted by the thres principles of *samyak jñāna, samyak darśana, and samyak caritra.*

Mahāvrata and Aṇuvrata

The Mahāvratas are the five great vows which Jain monks observe. They are:

Ahiṃsā (Nonviolence)

Satya (Truth)

Asteya (Non-stealing)

Brahmacarya (Chastity)

Aparigraha (Non-possession/Non-attachement)

For lay people, there is a corresponding set of five milder vows termed Anuvratas.

Doctrine of Karma

The doctrine of karma is of key importance in understanding the path of self-realisation as taught by Mahāvīra. The self or soul is considered to be pure. Karma is made up of very small material particles which are not perceptible with the senses. These particles of karma pollute the soul, thereby diminishing its purity. The contact of karma and soul causes the positive and negative experiences of life, further leading to the chain of birth and death.

Karmic particles become attracted to the soul as a result of one's behaviour. Depending upon the nature of the behaviour, the corresponding karma adheres to the soul. These karmas result in corresponding effects which the bearer of the karma has to face. The behaviour can be of mind, body or speech, and both intentional or unintentional.

Apart from its various effects, one of the main effects of karma is ignorance of one's true nature. The path to realising one's nature is to bear the results of one's karma with equanimity, thereby freeing *(Nirjarā)* oneself from all the accumulated karma. Upon totally freeing the soul from all the attached karma particles *(Mokṣa)*, the soul is experienced in its purest original form.

Meditations

As one progresses on the path of realisation, the following states of knowledge unfold sequentially, called Guṇasthānas. There are fourteen such steps:

1. The stage of the wrong believer (*mithyādṛṣṭi*)
2. The stage of one who has a slight taste of right belief (*sāsvādanasamyagdṛṣṭi*).
3. The stage of mixed belief (*miśradṛṣṭi*)
4. The stage of one who has true belief but does not yet have self-discipline (*avirata samyagdṛṣṭi*).
5. The stage of partial self-control (*deśavirata*)
6. The stage of complete self-discipline, although sometimes brought into wavering through negligence (*pramattasaṁyata*).
7. The stage of self-control without negligence (*apramattasaṁyata*)
8. The stage of one in whom the passions are still occurring in a gross form *(nivrtti bādara samparāya)*
9. The stage of one who practices the process called *anivratti karana* (the process of meditation through which the soul attains right belief or self-realisation by suppressing certain types of karmas) and in whom, however, the passions are still active *(anivṛtti bādara samparāya)*
10. The stage of one in whom the passions are active in a subtle form (*sūkṣma samparāya*)
11. The stage of one who has suppressed every passion but still does not possess omniscience (*upaśānta kaṣāya vītarāga chadmastha*)
12. The stage of who has annihilated every passion but does not yet possess omniscience (*kṣīna kaṣāya vitarāga chadmastha*).
13. The stage of omniscience with activity *(sayogi kevalin)*
14. The stage of omniscience without any activity *(ayogi kevalin)* (Jaini, 1998. Ch. 8)

The first four *guṇasthāna* are related to belief or rationality in perception. As and when the soul acquires rationality in perception, it moves on to 4th *guṇasthāna*. Stages 5 to 14 relate to conduct. Purity of conduct determines the *guṇasthāna* from 5th stage onwards.

As the individual progresses through each stage, ignorance fades owing to *nirjarā* and removal of karma from the soul. This also results in ashining of the knowledge that the soul possesses. The five types of knowledge thus emerge sequentially on the path of enlightenment.

The five Jñānas:

Matijñāna: The knowledge that is acquired by means of the senses and the intellect.

Śrutajñāna: The knowledge obtained through words, etc., from narration, *shastras*, etc.

Avadhijñāna: The knowledge of the things obtained by the soul, without the help of the mind or the senses (Extrasensory Perception).

Manaḥparyāyajñāna: The direct knowledge of the mind (telepathic knowledge) of the mental states and modifications of other humans.

Kevaljñāna: The total direct knowledge by the soul of all the *dravyas* and modifications in this universe.

Comprehensive and Synthetic approach

Mahāvīra stated that truth is manifold and our day-to-day language cannot fully express the ultimate truth. Truth expressed in language is essentially limited or partial. To understand the complete truth, one must enquire into all the aspects of truth. Holding only one particular aspect of truth as the whole truth is Ekāntavāda. It is similar to the story of six blind men trying to understand what the elephant is, and each man fighting with another as each of them perceived it differently depending on which part of elephant they were touching. To overcome this problem, Mahāvīra suggested the approach of Anekāntavāda. Anekāntavāda, with its offshoots of Syādavāda and Nayavāda, provides us with a method of systematically examining all the aspects of truth.

Thus, this way of looking at things leads to an understanding of truth which is comprehensive. It also creates a possibility of synthesising various views to form a common collective theory which can explain reality in a more holistic way. A greater discussion on this aspect of Anekāntavāda will appear in the final chapter on synthesis.

Concluding remarks

Are Mokṣa, Nirvāṇa and Keval Jñāna the same? Apparently, based on the description of these states by their advocates, they appear to be quite similar – the highest happiness and permanent freedom from the cycle of death and rebirth and its resultant sorrow. Theoretically, though, there are differences at a metaphysical level owing to the difference in the conception of the self in the Advaita, Buddhist and Jain systems. This will be dealt with in greater depth in the last chapters of this book.

Modern Indian Thought on Self

In the previous chapters, three prominent thinkers of ancient India were discussed. In the following chapters, the philosophy of three of modern India's influential thinkers will be discussed. We will examine whether the distance of 2500 years has any obvious impact on the expression of ideas related to self and self-realisation. By the twentieth century, both science and philosophy had experienced many new currents of thought and schools with radical new approaches to looking at self. By this time, many new disciplines, such as psychology, anthropology and sociology, along with the natural sciences, had developed various models of self and subjectivity and it was in this atmosphere that the philosophies of the three selected thinkers grew and were communicated to the audiences who naturally were intellectually far different to the audience of a couple of millennia previously. The thoughts of Buddha, Mahāvīra and Śaṅkara were brought to the attention of the Western mind only a couple of centuries ago, whereas, in modern times, the thought of Ramana Maharshi, Sri Aurobindo and J. Krishnamurti were simultaneously received by both the East and the West.

Ramana Maharshi

1879 –1950

*Your own Self-Realization is the greatest service
you can render to the world*

Chapter 7

Ramana Maharshi

BIOSKETCH

Born in the late 19th century in India, Ramana was a spiritual guru to thousands across the world. He lived a renunciate life in his ashram in south India. His teachings were simple yet profound and guided seekers to enquire into their true nature. Even today, hundreds of thousands of seekers across the world derive guidance and inspiration from the life and teachings of Ramana Maharshi.

Self and I

The word Brahman does not appear much in Ramana's teachings, indeed, quite infrequently in comparison with the word Self. For Ramana, Self is the only reality, the highest and the only absolute principle. Unlike Śaṅkara, who established the Brahman and then said 'I am that', Ramana reveals its true meaning as the 'Brahman exists as I'. There is a subtle difference between the two.

For Ramana, reality is a monistic principle and cannot be referred to in the second or third person. Unless we have the first person pronoun I, we cannot have the second and third person which, in turn, are dependent on the first person pronoun. For Ramana, this first person pronoun I is the only reality that exists. Reality (as historically denoted by the principle of Brahman) exists in first person, as I, as the Self which is One, a monistic subjective principle. Not merely is this the primary subject, there are no objects, and any appearance of objects is illusory. And, in fact, the source of everything can be found in the one and only reality, the Self – which can never be an object, thus cannot be known by anything else but itself.

Self-inquiry

Ramana's ideas related to Self can be understood in the following response of his to the question, 'What is the nature of the Self?'

> What exists in truth is the Self alone. The world, the individual soul and God are appearances in it. Like silver in mother-of-pearl, these three appear at the same time and disappear at the same time. The Self is that where there is absolutely no 'I-thought'. That is called 'Silence'. The Self itself is the world; the Self itself is 'I'; the Self itself is God; all is Siva, the Self. (Maharshi, 1968).

As everything is really the Self, one naturally thinks that the only thing to realise is the Self. Regarding Self-realisation, Ramana says that Self always remains real, so there is no need to real-ise it. He says it is the unreal world of objects and forms that we have real-ised by falling prey to false notions and it such errors that we need to rectify and to un-realise the world.

Identification with body

Ramana says, the entire Vedantic scriptures' essence is *'Deham naham. Koham? Soham'. Dehabuddhi,* or, the belief that I am body is the reason for all suffering and illusion. Once it is realised that I am not the body, but the eternal principle through *jñāna drishti,* one is liberated. What is bondage and how does it come into being? Self, which is pure undivided consciousness, appears to be individual (*jīva*). The *jīva* is the reflected consciousness (*cidbhāsa*). It is here that the first concept of I, the ego, emerges. This is the source of all other concepts, and also what we can call the mind. Mind or ego has no form of its own but it assumes the form of whatever it holds on to. Thus, in the absence of all thoughts and concepts, there is no mind, thus no ego. It is the mind which projects itself outward, creating the world of phenomena.

States of consciousness

Although the consciousness is one, there are typically three states experienced by all: waking, dreaming and deep sleep. The phenomenal world, with all its forms, exists in the waking and dream states which depend on the ego. In deep sleep, there is no ego or I and individual consciousness disappears.

The fourth state – the *thuriya*

The fourth state is possible for a realised person which is beyond the three states experienced by all. This is the state of wakefulness, but devoid of ego, where the consciousness is One and everything is perceived as Self. In fact, from the layman's perspective, it is *thuriya*. But for the *Jnani* it is *thuriyateeta* or beyond *thuriya*, as, for the *Jñāni*, there is a realisation that the consciousness was ever present and the divisive states of wakefulness, dream and deep sleep never existed.

The path to self-realisation

Although the concept of bondage and liberation are discussed in Ramana's teachings, he makes it clear that these concepts are mere concepts and for a *Jñāni* they are non-existent. There is no bondage; how, therefore, can there be liberation? Yet, perhaps for the ones who do have notions of path and goal, there are various paths that Ramana spoke of:

They are *stuti, japa, dhyāna, yoga*, and *Jñāna*

Stuti is singing the praises of the Lord with a great feeling of devotion.

Japa is uttering the names of the gods or sacred mantras such as Om either mentally or verbally. He explains that, while following the methods of *stuti* and *japa,* the mind will sometimes be concentrated and sometimes diffused. The tendencies of mind cannot be understood by practicing the above methods.

Dhyāna denotes the repetition of the names, etc., mentally (*japa*) with feelings of devotion. In this method, he said, the state of the mind is understood easily. *Dhyāna* can make the mind still.

Perfection in *dhyāna* is the state of abiding in the Self, according to Ramana.

Yoga: The source of the breath is the same as that of the mind; therefore the subsidence of either leads effortlessly to that of the other. The practice of stilling the mind through breath control (*prānayāma*) is called yoga.

Jñāna is the annihilation of the mind in which it is made to assume the form of the Self through the constant practice of *dhyāna* or enquiry (*vicāra*). The extinction of the mind is the state in which there is a cessation of all effort. Those who are established in this state never swerve from their true state. The terms 'silence' (*mauna*) and inaction refer to this highest state. In Ramana's words,

> Those who follow the path of enquiry realise that the mind which remains at the end of the enquiry is Brahman. Those who practise meditation realise that the mind which remains at the end of the meditation is the object of their meditation. As the result is the same in either case, it is the duty of aspirants to practise continuously either of these methods until the goal has been reached." (Maharshi, 2004).

Self-enquiry

There is a clear hierarchy in the paths. The one meant for the ripe souls, the highest and the final path is that of enquiry: who am I? This distinctly highlights Ramana's philosophy and what can be regarded as his one point teaching to all who wanted to realise the true nature of self. When asked, *"How will the mind become quiescent?"*, Ramana answered, "By the enquiry 'Who am I?'. The thought 'Who am I?' will destroy all other thoughts, and like the stick used for stirring the burning pyre, it will itself in the end be destroyed. Then, there will arise Self-realisation." (Maharshi, 1968)

Meditation or *dhyāna* is something that can prepare the mind for the enquiry by silencing the mind. Although such mind remains silent only until the thoughts are kept under control by concentration on any object or controlling the breath. The enquiry into the very nature of self was something that Ramana proposed would destroy the ego and simultaneously make one realise who one is. Upon asking about every thought, that who does this thought occur to (including to the thoughts which are answers to this question), one's attention can be drawn inward towards the self and, on again asking who this I is, one can arrive at the realisation that the Self remains as pure awareness.

Thus, by guidance through practices and elucidating the philosophy of Self, Ramana, through his life and the books based on his answers to questioners from all walks of life, embodied and guided others to the eternal truth of the *sat citānanda*, ever existing as Self.

Sri Aurobindo

1872 –1950

The one aim of my yoga is an inner self-development
by which each one who follows it can in time discover
the One Self in all

Chapter 8

Sri Aurobindo

Nominated for both the Nobel Peace Prize and the Nobel Prize in Literature, Aurobindo was an outstanding scholar, philosopher, poet and spiritual master of high calibre. He was born in British India. He renounced his career as a political rebel to lead a spiritual life. He wrote extensively on philosophy and religion and created his philosophy of integral yoga which gave a new vision of the transformation of human nature. Aurobindo has inspired countless people all over the world and his work continues through his voluminous books, an ashram in south India, as well as the modern world international town of Auroville.

Before we focus our discussion on Aurobindo's conception of self, we will take a look at his view of reality. According to Aurobindo, these two processes show the movement of existence: involution and evolution.

Process of creation and evolution

According to Aurobindo, there are two central movements in the process of creation: an involution of consciousness from an original omnipresent Reality, manifesting a universe of forms, including matter; and an evolution of those material forms in creation upward toward life, mind, and spirit, reconnecting to their spiritual source.

Involution

Sri Aurobindo refers to the process by which the Energy of creation emerged from a timeless, spaceless, ineffable, immutable Reality, as the Involution. According to him, the nature of Reality is *Satcidānanda*. Sometimes, he also uses the term Brahman for this. As one can see in the following text, the nature of this Reality is not different from that of Śaṅkara. However, there are some differences. According to his theory of creation, Brahman extends itself to Being/Existence (*Sat*), which generated a force of Consciousness (*Cit*), and Bliss (*Ānanda*) self-enjoyment in existing and being conscious. Through the action of a fourth dimension, *Supermind* (i.e., Truth Consciousness), the Force (Cit) of *Sat-Cit-Ānanda* was divided into Knowledge and Will, eventually formulating as an invisible Energy that would become the source of creation. Through its own wilful self-absorption of consciousness, the universe would begin as unconscious material existence from out of that Energy.

Evolution

The process of existence emerging out of the unconscious is referred to as evolution. Initially, it emerges gradually in the stages of matter, life, and mind. First, matter evolves from simple to complex forms. Then, life emerges in matter and evolves from simple to complex forms. Finally, mind emerges in life and evolves from rudimentary to higher forms of thought and reason. As each new principle emerges, the previous stages remain but are integrated into the higher principle. Humanity represents the stage of development of mind in complex material forms of life.

This higher evolution is described as a dual movement; inward, away from surface consciousness and into the depths, culminating in the realisation of the Psychic Being (the personal evolving soul); and then upward to the higher levels of spiritual mind (the Higher Mind, Illumined Mind, Intuitive Mind, and Overmind), culminating in the final stage of supramentalisation. Whereas these higher levels of consciousness have been attained in particular individuals, they must eventually emerge more universally as general stages in evolution. When they do emerge, this will result in the embodiment of a new species on earth that will be once again united in consciousness with *satcidānanda*.

Thus, one can note that, in the ongoing process of evolution, humans are by no means at the final stage. The journey of matter back to life and the Divine is what marks the future of our evolution, according to Aurobindo.

In the scheme of things, when we look at the individual, this individual, in turn, is made up of several hierarchical levels: vital, physical, mental and psychic.

Triple transformation

The evolution of the individual is marked by the following steps, known as the triple transformation:

Psychic Transformation - The first of the three stages is a movement within, away from the surface of life, to the depths, culminating in the discovery of one's psychic being (the evolving soul). From that experience, one sees the oneness and unity of creation, and the harmony of all opposites experienced in life.

Spiritual Transformation - As a result of making the psychic change, one's mind expands and s/he experiences knowledge not through the hard churning of thought, but through light, intuition, and revelation of knowledge, culminating in supramental perception. Light enters from the heights and begins to transmute various parts of one's being.

Supramental Transformation - After making the psychic and spiritual change, one makes the *supramental* and the most radical change. It is basically a complete transformation of the mind, the heart, the emotions, and the physical body.

Supramental

Sri Aurobindo's vision of the future includes the appearance of what may be called a new species, the *supramental* being, a divine being which would be as different and superior to present humanity as humanity is to the animal kingdom. It would have a consciousness different in kind to the mind of the human, a different status and quality and functionality. Even the physical form of this being would be different, more luminous and flexible and adaptable, entirely conscious and harmonious. Between this *supramental* being and humanity, there would be transitional beings, who would be human in birth and form, but whose consciousness would approach that of the *supramental* being. These transitional beings would appear prior to that of the full *supramental* being, and would constitute an intermediate stage in the Earth's evolution, through which the soul would pass in its growth towards its divine manifestation as the *supramental* being in the earth nature.

As is evident in the description above, individual self-realisation or spiritual enlightenment is not the last stop in Aurobindo's scheme of things. What he saw was the evolution of all mankind which will begin with a few but will have to spread to the entire society, changing the very way we live our lives, ushering in a new age, the crucial next step in evolution.

This process is attained by not just one's own efforts, but, in a parallel way, there is grace too which pours down into matter to help create a bridge between the present and the future of the individual. Nevertheless, without focusing much on the future vision of man, we shall restrict our discussion to an examination of the role of self and the process of self-realisation.

As we can see in Aurobindo's Integral Yoga, we find a rich description of self with its various aspects and sub-aspects. The path to realising this self typically follows the steps of: aspiration, rejection and surrender.

Practices

Aurobindo's Integral Yoga does not prescribe any specific practice. Upon surrendering to the deeper and higher principle, it is one's intuition which is supposed to guide the person.

In the later chapters, where several issues related to self and self-realisation will be dealt with simultaneously by bringing together relevant aspects of all the philosophies, we shall further critically examine the principles of self and self-realisation in Integral Yoga as proposed by Aurobindo.

J. Krishnamurti

1895 –1986

Self-knowledge has no end – you don't come to an
achievement, you don't come to a conclusion. It is an
endless river

Chapter 9

J. Krishnamurti

BIOSKETCH

Named by Time magazine as one of the five saints of the 20th century, Krishnamurti was identified and raised to be a world teacher by the Theosophical Society. He later renounced the title and spent his entire life travelling across the world engaging with audiences and sharing his insights into human freedom. He rejected all forms of formal religions, systems and authorities. Krishnamurti's teachings continue to influence many scholars, educators, scientists and seekers.

Krishnamurti is considered as one of the most significant thinkers of the twentieth century. Through his books, talks and dialogues with scholars, religious leaders, scientists and people from all walks of life, his teachings echoed over seventy years. There are several nuances in his philosophy which, in essence, focused on everyday problems of living, such as violence, fear, relationships, desire and death.

Role of Authority

Krishnamurti did not believe in any authority when it came to finding the truth of life. In fact, one of the core aspects of his philosophy is that assuming any authority is a sure hindrance to finding truth. To Krishnamurti, understanding of and freedom from self was the essential function of human life. So here we have a philosophy which rejected any reference to the scriptures, just like Mahāvīra and Buddha, and insisted that individuals have to find truth for themselves.

Self-understanding

Krishnamurti's approach to understanding personal and social life was based on a complete understanding of actual phenomena. And one needs to be free of the past to understand what is unfolding in the present, for truth, he said is not a static thing, but a living reality which can be understood by a being who is free from all past knowledge.

The phenomena can be explained in terms of sensation, i.e., the stimuli which enter through the senses and are perceived by the brain. These stimuli interact with previously stored memories and their categories, leading to recognition of the stimuli and their nomenclature. Thus, based on such mental conditioning, which is an ongoing process from past generations, there is a conditioned response in the form of desire, often influenced by ideals created by authorities and sustained by the continuous process of movement of thought in a conditioned pattern towards becoming the ideal that it projects. Thus, all human activities are conditioned responses. These limiting conditioned responses are the essence of bondage and the eternal quest for freedom. This is also the source of the notion of time. The movement of thought and its fragmentary nature continued through memories gives rise to the notion of time, with all the thinking essentially based on the past, including the projected images of the future, creating a sense of time. For Krishnamurti, thought, memory and time were synonymous.

Choiceless awareness

When one tries to observe these phenomena, one encounters with the content of one's own consciousness. Krishnamurti questions the existence of an observer independent of the object of observation – the observed. For Krishnamurti, the observer, often perceived as self or I, is just another thought. For there is no self separate from the things it is observing. All categories fall into the realms of thought, including the one which is artificially separated as self or observer. Thus, when there is a clear perception that the observer is the observed, duality can end instantaneously. This has to be an action beyond the realm of thoughts, thus, not of time.

> It is only when one is in contact, when there is no space between the observer and the observed that one is in total relationship.. when there is this complete absence of space as the observer and the observed, then there is vast space. In that space there is no conflict; in that space there is freedom. Freedom is not a reaction. You cannot say, 'Well, I am free'. The moment you say you are free you are not free, because you are conscious of yourself as being free from something, and therefore

you have the same situation as an observer observing a tree. He has created a space, and in that space he breeds conflict. To understand this requires not intellectual agreement or disagreement, or saying, 'I don't understand', but rather it requires coming directly into contact with what is. It means seeing that all your actions, every moment of action is of the observer and the observed, and within that space there is pleasure, pain and suffering, the desire to fulfil, to become famous. Within that space there is no contact with anything. Contact, relationship has a quite different meaning when the observer is no longer apart from the observed. There is this extraordinary space, and there is freedom. (Krishnamurti, 1995).

It is this freedom from knowledge that can truly free a person to experience what can be only denoted but never captured by words such as love, beauty or sacred. Krishnamurti does not describe this reality, neither does he assert that that is the absolute or otherwise, as any discussion about it merely falls into the realm of thought which is limited, and thus, by definition, not what it is attempting to describe.

Truth as a pathless land

What sets Krishnamurti apart from most thinkers was the radical stance that no method and no authority of any sort can help an individual to see the truth. In fact, the very reason for suffering and bondage is the very striving and the movement of thought in order to achieve an imagined goal by an imagined self. For Krishnamurti, human existence was essentially that of interrelatedness. In his words, 'to be is to be related'. In fact, he stated there is no difference between the self and the world, 'you are the world and the world is you'. The thought that separates itself as self and calls other thoughts world, can both be seen as mere ideas which transform when there is a perception that the observer is the observed, thus the self and world are but one.

Krishnamurti emphasised that 'truth is a pathless land', elaborating that no method, no belief can take an individual to the truth, for truth is not static, but a living reality to be perceived not through the past, but with a mind that is free from the self. For Krishnamurti, such understanding was instant and could not be turned into a goal to be achieved through time, through practice, for any such mental activity will but strengthen the divide between what is and what should be, thus continuing and fuelling the divisive action of thought, creating identities and further fragmentation of energy. This idea that no path can lead to truth is explained in the following words from Krishnamurti:

> When you speak of a path to truth, it implies that truth, this living reality, is not in the present, but somewhere in the distance, somewhere in the future. Now to me, truth is fulfilment, and to fulfilment there can be no path. So it seems, to me at least, that the first illusion in which you are caught is this desire for assurance, this desire for certainty, this inquiry after a path, a way, a mode of living whereby you can attain the desired goal, which

is truth. Your conviction that truth exists only in the distant future implies imitation. When you inquire what truth is, you are really asking to be told the path which leads to truth. Then you want to know which system to follow, which mode, which discipline, to help you on the way to truth. But to me there is no path to truth; truth is not to be understood through any system, through any path. A path implies a goal, a static end, and therefore a conditioning of the mind and the heart by that end, which necessarily demands discipline, control, acquisitiveness. This discipline, this control, becomes a burden; it robs you of freedom and conditions your action in daily life. Inquiry after truth implies a goal, a static end, which you are seeking. And that you are seeking a goal shows that your mind is searching for assurance, certainty. To attain this certainty, mind desires a path, a system, a method which it can follow, and this assurance you think to find by conditioning mind and heart through self-discipline, self-control, suppression. But truth is a reality that cannot be understood by following any path. Truth is not a conditioning, a shaping of the mind and heart, but a constant fulfilment, a fulfilment in action. That you inquire after truth implies that you believe in a path to truth, and this is the first illusion in which you are caught.

Meditation

According to Krishnamurti, meditation, not as a method but as a way of being, held the key. For meditation, for him, was emptying of mind. When there is no identification with any thought as me or self, then mind naturally empties itself, altering the very way of existence, creating a freedom in which the body and mechanical thought go on functioning, but without the sense of self, self being a thought which is absent in meditation.

As one can see, there are no scriptures, no authority and no methods or practices in this approach. There is simply an understanding and perception which alters one's way of living, not as a result of a sustained belief over a period of time but a total perception in the present moment revealing the illusory nature of the self and its conditioning, resulting in emptying of the mind, creating freedom beyond and from time.

Krishnamurti cautioned people against accepting any spiritual authority. He pointed out the danger in accepting any authority and urged people to see that accepting any authority stems merely from seeking security and cannot help in discovering the true nature of self, which is the most important function of a human being. He speaks on authority:

> We listen with hope and fear; we seek the light
> of another but are not alertly passive to be able
> to understand. If the liberated seems to fulfil
> our desires we accept him; if not, we continue
> our search for the one who will; what most
> of us desire is gratification at different levels.
> What is important is not how to recognize

one who is liberated but how to understand yourself. No authority here or hereafter can give you knowledge of yourself; without self-knowledge there is no liberation from ignorance, from sorrow.

Concluding Remarks on the modern thinkers

To sum up, in this section, in the first part, the key concepts from Ramana's works, like the difference between Self and I, the method of Self-inquiry, the results of identification with the body, the states of consciousness and different methods of self-realisation, viz., *stuti, japa, dhyāna, yoga* and *jñāna*, were discussed. Subsequently, Aurobindo's ideas related to the process of creation (involution and evolution), the steps of triple transformation, consisting of psychic, spiritual and *supramental* transformation, were discussed, followed by a discussion on thoughts on practices prescribed in Integral Yoga. Later, Krishnamurti's key teachings were discussed.

In the next section, the varied theories of self and self-realisation discussed and elaborated in last two sections will be analysed on various parameters. Looking at all these theories simultaneously, and discovering the emerging threads of similarities and differences, and the practical implications of these approaches, they will be juxtaposed and analysed critically, while keeping the focus on theories and practices of self and self-realisation.

Critical and Comparative Account

Chapter 10

Critical Résumé

Ancient Indian Thinkers

Śaṅkara

Just as Advaita Vedānta is essentially full of the glory of and emphasis on Brahman and its sole existence, we observe that, as a consequence, thoughts and guidance related to everyday life, ethics, and the details of the path towards self-realisation are not talked about at great length. A lot of emphasis is also placed on denying the contrary ideologies. As we saw in the earlier chapter, this was one of the primary goals of Śaṅkara.

Overall, in Advaita Vedānta, Śaṅkara vehemently puts forth the idea of all-pervading Brahman and its sole existence. Inasmuch as he asserts the presence of this eternal principle which is the self or atman, with equal emphasis he denies the existence of the material world, calling it *māyā* or delusion. Ignorance or *avidyā*, which results in false perception, can be replaced by true understanding and realisation of *"Sarvam khalu idam Brahma"* and, finally, the self-realisation that I am Brahman, *"Aham brahmāsmi"* which is sat cit ānanda or joyful conscious existence.

Buddha

Just as Śaṅkara's theory - which rejects the world - comes under massive attack, so do the Buddha's theories, on account of his complete denial of self or soul. Especially when Buddha talks about the concepts of rebirth and karma, which are significant to Buddha's teachings, questions naturally arise regarding what it is that undergoes birth and death. Such criticisms are handled in several places in Buddhist literature by scholars such as Nagarjuna, etc. What can be seen as a significant differentiator in Advaitins and Buddhist thought is that, in Buddhism, we find a greater focus on the individual and a detailed outline of the path that leads to *nirvāṇa*. The daunting questions do remain about whose *nirvāṇa* or whose realisation Śaṅkara and Buddha were talking about. To common sense, these can be clear, but philosophically both theories need to assert the individual, whether an illusion of *māyā* or a mere *saṅghata* of conditioned phenomena. After all, it is the same subject that they are talking about: who can attain the states of oneness with *satcidānanda* Brahman or the final peace of *nirvāṇa*.

Mahāvīra

Mahāvīra, based on the principle of Anekāntavāda, took a more inclusive stance. The soul in its ideal state is infinite. This infiniteness of soul is not in terms of size or shape, but in terms of its knowledge, intuition, bliss and energy. However, owing to the contact with the karmic *pudgalas* it becomes limited, thus creating a transient reality. As Mahāvīra did not take a stance similar to Śaṅkara, who asserted the sole existence of an infinite principle, or like Buddha, who denied any such substance, Mahāvīra's teachings were attacked by all other schools, especially on account of not stating a single omnipresent principle. Mahāvīra's anekāntavāda was often perceived as hesitant in taking any ideological stance.

In this chapter, all of these theories will be analysed to reveal their similarities and differences by focusing on key attributes.

Modern Indian Thinkers

The advantage in studying these thinkers from recent years is that, unlike the historical thinkers in whose case we have only a number of texts which were written as poetry and passed on from generation to generation, in recent times, we have authentic sources of these thinkers' biographies. It has also been possible to capture their thoughts and philosophies by advanced means of recording technology, in some cases, even with audio and video. A lot of material that we refer to in studying these thinkers has been published in their lifetimes and thus approved and authorised by the thinkers themselves. Unfortunately, this is not the case with any of the three thinkers from ancient India. In the cases of Mahāvīra and Buddha, they did not write. The disciples captured their teachings and passed them on in oral traditions, often converting the teachings into poetic sutras. This invariably influenced the format of the material composed, in the sense that it had to be easy to memorise. The writing was done much later, presumably after changes in the original. Although there is historical evidence indicating that Buddhist disciples took great care to adhere to the original teachings, there is no doubt amongst academics that the scriptures do not represent a verbatim account of Buddha's teachings. Similar questions also remain in relation to the other two thinkers. There are writings which are attributed to Śaṅkara, which remain informed guesses, without the possibility of definite assertion that they were indeed written by him. Nevertheless, there is substantial proof that these rich philosophies were indeed propagated by these thinkers with their unique stances on self and self-realisation giving rise not only to distinct schools of philosophy, but also to traditions and practices which have continued to evolve until our own times, influencing every aspect of religious, moral, social and political life in India and beyond.

Ramana

With reference to Śaṅkara's philosophy, one can see clearly that Ramana's teaching fitted very well with Advaita Vedānta's doctrine. We find Ramana often referring to the *Śrutis* and definitely propagating Advaita Vedantic thought. This being the case, there are nevertheless several unique features in Ramana's teachings. Although, to a philosophical reader, some of his teachings may sound similar to the traditional ones, there were unique differences and his definite emphasis becomes very clear to the reader as one sees an exhaustive account of his conversations with various seekers over a few decades.

In Ramana's teachings, we find a clear focus on Self. Having studied Śaṅkara, one may erroneously equate both these people's teachings, but, in doing so, although not a logical error, one may miss the very explanation that Ramana gives for his philosophy. For example, it is widely known that Śaṅkara denied the existence of the world. Ramana, in his own words, said that it is not true that Śaṅkara denied the existence of the world. Ramana asserts that the world exists, but it exists as Brahman and said that this is what Śaṅkara meant. Although Ramana seems to accept the authority of Vedantic texts and clearly favours Advaita Vedānta, there were several points on which he did not hesitate to differ and give his own twist to the theories.

Having said that, a unique problem with Advaita Vedantic theories remains, and it remains even in the case of Ramana, viz., the only reality they accept and consider to be the one and only thing that exists is by nature formless and indescribable, leaving any attempts at their description of the subject to dangers of contraction. A reader may therefore become confused when different categories, such as eternal and transient, real and unreal, etc., are put forth, the path defined and certain goals like mokṣa upheld, as all categories, forms and differentiations are unreal and there exists no individual in the ultimate scheme of things. Calling the individual self a mere illusion suddenly puts all teachings into the category of *māyā* or illusion. In fact, for the realised *jnani*, there is no illusion, no path, no striving, no *avidyā*. If we look carefully, one might find oneself caught up in a loop of non-provable arguments.

Perhaps for this reason, Ramana stated that intellectual endeavours or discussions and reading were fundamentally unnecessary. Ramana was asked, "Is it any use reading books for those who long for release? All the texts say that in order to gain release one should?" To which Ramana's responds:

Render the mind quiescent; therefore their conclusive teaching is that the mind should be rendered quiescent; once this has been understood there is no need for endless reading. In order to quieten the mind one has only to inquire within oneself what one's Self is; how could this search be done in books? One should know one's Self with one's own eye of wisdom. The Self is within the five sheaths; but books are outside them. Since the Self has to be inquired into by discarding the five sheaths, it is futile to search for it in books. There will come a time when one will have to forget all that one has learned.

Similarly when a questioner asked Ramana about the importance of studying certain aspects of philosophy, Ramana's answer clarifies his emphasis on empirical work and his disregard for sheer intellectual efforts. When specifically asked if it was necessary for one who longs for release to inquire into the nature of categories (tattvas), Ramana answered:

Just as one who wants to throw away garbage has no need to analyse it and see what it is, so one who wants to know the Self has no need to count the number of categories or inquire into their characteristics; what he has to do is to reject altogether the categories that hide the Self. The world should be considered like a dream.

He often upheld that it is in silence that the truth can be conveyed and not through words. Yet, through the account of a lifetime of conversations, we do see a unique understanding of self and self-realisation that Ramana drew people's attention to. Seers like Ramana often disregard intellectual debates. Their emphasis is on experience – the experience of the absolute which is beyond the capacity of words to describe. Ramana, through his words, tried to lead people to experience this blissful silence.

Aurobindo

Sri Aurobindo (1872 – 1950) took Indian philosophy to a new destination. Aurobindo spent almost all of his later years producing voluminous works, later to be published as a series of volumes in the collected works series. In these texts, we find a unique interpretation of the Vedas and Upaniṣads, along with his very original vision of self, universe and the Divine. The uniqueness of Aurobindo's work comes from several angles. In my view, two such aspects are most important. First, Aurobindo reviewed ancient Indian Vedic philosophy and practices from a theoretical as well as a socio-cultural point of view and integrated several aspects of different paths, giving new meaning to ancient concepts, and creating what he called Integral Yoga. Secondly, although based on the old foundation of Indian thought, he proposed an altogether new theory of the future evolution of man which definitely went beyond the much-discussed themes of ancient Indian philosophy. Aurobindo's philosophy of self and self-realisation is a key aspect which we will focus on, which essentially touches upon all the important concepts in his theory and practice.

Although Aurobindo seems to be in line with the concept of Brahman as traditionally understood, he refused to call the world an illusion. In accepting the absolute, he was not willing to compromise on the individual existence of people in a physical world. In fact, as we will see in the following, Aurobindo goes to great lengths to explain different aspects and levels of being, followed by his grand vision for the evolution of life on earth.

In summary, the Integral Yoga of Aurobindo bases itself on the absolute *sat cit ānanda* Brahman, respects and acknowledge individual existence of human and also the world of matter, and aspires and inspires humans to evolve in creating a new universe where matter is transformed and reflects the absolute Brahman, resulting in a harmonious society governed by the psychic, in spite of the present human race which is more under the influence of vital and mental processes. The theory has inspired a lot of research and disciplines devoted to studying its various postulates under the disciplines of Integral Yoga and Integral Psychology.

Due to its very inclusive notions, this theory, so vast, and appealingly choosing a middle path with regard to all philosophical notions, does escape criticism. Although any strict monist or idealist will criticise this theory as rather weak in its stance and, in particular, will question its explanations regarding the transformation of the formless into forms and the explanation of future superhumans who will live freely in spite of the problems of current divisible existence, such criticism is definitely not more severe than that which is raised against the purist theories as discussed in the case of Śaṅkara and Buddha.

Aurobindo receives credit for his attempts to describe in detail various levels of existence. He also links these levels to his overall utopian idea of the evolution of mankind into a race of

superhumans. His notion of the future is hard to prove or disprove, as it is a speculation. As regards the path of self-realisation,
Aurobindo's theory cannot be put into any specific category. He
does advocate *sādhanā* but it is not of any particular kind. Nor does
he take a stance like that of Buddha or Mahāvir, wherein individual emancipation relies on one's own efforts alone. Aurobindo's
path speaks about individual aspiration as well as Divine Grace.
There is a strong deterministic element in his theory, coupled with
an emphasis on entire *humanity* as against a focus on individuals.
This separates his theory from the rest. Being a very collectivistic,
diverse and deterministic theory, it does lose its edge in giving a
focussed view on the important concepts of self and self-realisation. Instead, what we have is a rich multifaceted projection.

Aurobindo, too, would perhaps agree with these comments,
as, towards the end of his life, he stated that he would like to be
remembered as a poet (not a philosopher).

J. Krishnamurti

Of the six thinkers in this book, Krishnamurti stands apart
from the rest in many regards. All the other thinkers include
many esoteric concepts in their theories, such as that of rebirth,
etc. They all also rely on belief in certain principles which are
foundational to their teachings. Krishnamurti made no references
to any of the scriptures. Nor did he use any concept or idea which
is not immediately perceptible to us. In fact, he cautioned against
believing in any dogmas or promises that such theories offer.

Krishnamurti's approach to understanding self is straightforward and based on observing oneself. He does not deny anything

that one experiences, nor does he assert anything that is not perceptible. Krishnamurti's teachings can be readily tested against one's own experience without subscribing to any set of beliefs. This is a clear strength of his teachings. Because Krishnamurti bases his teachings on everyday experience and highlights the importance of watching 'what is', there is nothing to prove wrong in terms of any theoretical assumptions or principles, as there are none.

The self as described by Krishnamurti is empirical and phenomenological. It can be experienced by everyone. The enquiry into the roots of the self leads one to realise the origin of such self in the past. Upon observing the whole movement of this self in the mechanism of thought, one is freed from it. In comparison with the others, Krishnamurti's is the most simple, logical and straightforward approach, devoid of any unnecessary notions.

Chapter 11

Subjectivity and Self:
Empirical and Metaphysical

Having given a critical summary of the views as regards to self and self-realisation of these key thinkers, they will now be critically analysed and compared with particular reference to certain themes. Although the theories are different, one cannot assume that they are totally different from one another. There are some stark differences and then there are compelling similarities. This chapter aims to identify these similarities and differences and, by dissecting their sources, to lay the foundations for the derivation of important factors which may determine the essence of Indian thought on self and self-realisation as captured by the selected thinkers.

Subjectivity

Putting philosophical notions aside, any common person would agree that he or she has a sense of subjectivity or selfhood.

This is sometimes referred to as identity. In psychology, the branch of developmental psychology studies the distinct stages of human development, as defined by certain attributes. It is in early childhood that the child starts recognizing that it is not merely one of the objects that it encounters in the environment, but a specific subject, and the sense of self or I begins to emerge and strengthen. This sense of 'me' is universal to all humanity and no one would deny the existence of the active notion of 'I', 'me' and 'myself' in their life.

At an empirical level, we cannot deny the existence of self. In fact, the entire Western Enlightenment has made this self the centre and given it central importance either through experience, thinking or the very being, as emphasized by the empiricists, the rationalists and the existentialists. It is thus important to analyse this subject thoroughly before we merely philosophise certain premises as discussed in previous chapters, wherein some schools tend to deny the individual self on account of either permanence or impermanence.

Empirical and Metaphysical Self

The self, experienced as 'I', the first person pronoun, is common to all humans. It is in early childhood that this identity develops where the child recognises itself as different from everything else. This self is the empirical self. The self that many thinkers in this book talk about is the 'self' referred to as a noun. This is the metaphysical self.

It is often noticed that philosophers take a leap from empirical to metaphysical (pronoun to noun). Buddha, as well as Krishnamurti, refused to take such leap.

Almost all the other theories described in the previous chapters seem to find a common way to address this gulf between the daily practical empirical encounter with self and the metaphysical self which is only realised at the end of the path. (The discussion pertaining to the path, viz. self-realisation, will be addressed in much detail in the next section). Thus, the way out for many theories is to find a dual way of explaining things:

Śaṅkara

In Advaita, even though the existence of individual self is denied, there is a whole discourse based on the *Vyavahārika sattā* – the illusory empirical world. The self and its attributes appear only in *Vyavahārika* or *Pratibhāṣika Sattā*. *Pratibhāṣika Sattā* is the plane of dream reality which disappears as soon as one wakes up. In the 92nd verse of the Śataśloki, Śaṅkara explains how different attributes or components of self are non-real.

> 'I am neither the body nor the senses, nor the erratic mind, nor reason, nor life, nor the ego, nor wife, nor offspring, nor kith and kin, nor land, nor wealth and so on. How can I - who is the sole witness, pure consciousness, the inner self - be these things which are purely objective. I am the Supreme which is the reality behind this universe.' (Śataśloki: 92).

It is in the plane of *Paramārthikasattā* of absolute reality where the empirical world is revealed as the creation of māyā and ignorance.

Buddha

Although Buddha denies the permanent self, as we have seen in the previous chapters, the teaching is addressed towards the individuals who need to work out their own *Nirvāṇa*. Who are these individuals, monks and nuns? They are the result of *skandhas* which, as a result of *avidyā*, make them believe in the permanent self.

The Buddha taught that an individual is a combination of five aggregates of existence, also called the Five *Skandhas* or the five heaps. These are:

Rūpa (external and internal matter): Externally, *Rūpa* is the physical world. Internally, *Rūpa* includes the material body and the physical sense organs.

Sensation (feeling): sensing an object as either pleasant or unpleasant or neutral

Perception, Conception, Apperception, Cognition or discrimination: registers whether an object is recognized or not (for instance, the sound of a bell or the shape of a tree)

Mental formations, impulses, volition, or compositional factors: all types of mental habits, thoughts, ideas, opinions, prejudices, compulsions, and decisions triggered by an object.

Consciousness or discernment: a series of rapidly changing interconnected discrete acts of cognizance.

Though the Buddha denied metaphysical (permanent) self, he did not deny empirical self which is expressed by the pronoun 'I'. In his teachings, he did caution his disciples and cautioned them not to misuse this notion in day-to-day practicalities. One cannot engage in day-to-day dealings unless we recognize the continuity of the self, even if it is illusory. Thus, a monk (a continued self) is expected to follow *Śila* (conduct) and practice *Samādhi*, i.e., meditation and awaken his *Prajñā* or wisdom. At a practical level,

Buddha does recognize the human individual, even though, in the strictest sense, there is no individual, as in the case of the famous story of the chariot where Nāgasena explains to king Milinda that just as a chariot is not any of its particular parts, but is only a name that we ascribe to the whole complex of parts, similarly, the person too is not any of its particular parts; it is only a name that we ascribe to the complex of parts taken as a whole. The whole dialogue appears in the text of Milindapañha.

This is further substantiated by the use of certain words by Buddha, such as 'self-reliance' or 'self-illumination'. Buddha advised people to look within for all the support. *'Attā hi attāno nātho'*, meaning 'One is one's own refuge'. Another well-known teaching of Buddha is *'Attadipa viharatha, attasarana Anannasarana'*, meaning 'Be the light unto yourself, take refuge in yourself and no one else'. The use of the word *'attā'* here definitely does not mean soul or the Self as described in the Vedantas. Nevertheless, the term self is used purely to indicate the practical empirical self as commonly experienced. Evidently, Buddha does recognize the self at this level.

To assert this point further, the notion of two truths that appears in Buddhist literature can be helpful. The truth based on our everyday understanding is termed *samvrti-satya*. This is used for the communication of the practical aspects of life. This is the empirical reality,. whereas the *paramārtha-satya* is the ultimate truth. This is truth that is of an absolute nature, which lies beneath empirical experience. This, being the all-encompassing absolute truth, cannot be expressed in language. On the other hand, the *samvrti-satya* is something which is easily grasped, as it is based on everyday language. Thus, we can see that the discourse of self and self-realisation too needs to be understood depending upon whether they are held from the lower truth, i.e., *saṃvṛti-satya* or the higher truth, i.e., *paramārtha-satya*.

Mahāvīra

The acceptance of reality at different levels is perhaps most defined and pronounced in Jain thought. According to a dominant interpretation, Mahāvīra's thought should be understood from two standpoints: *Vyavahāranaya* (practical standpoint) and *Niścayanaya* (decisive or ultimate standpoint). This applies to the Jaina concept of *jīva* (self) as well. So, although the soul or *jīva* is infinite (that is, it has four infinities – those of knowledge, intuition, bliss and energy), such a description is valid when we look at the 'self' from *Niścayanaya*. Whereas, by *Vyavahāranaya*, Jainism accepts the existence of a finite individual with its accumulated Karma, resulting in various effects which are applicable to that specific individual. Accordingly, that *jīva* is in bondage, is just an empirical practical truth. In its true or ultimate nature, *jīva* is liberated.

Ramana

Much of the explanation above related to Śaṅkara is also applicable to Ramana, as their philosophical viewpoints are one and the same. Although the expression of Advaita, in case of Ramana, may have been certainly different to that of Śaṅkara, their essential philosophical standpoints were declaredly similar.

The main difference was in their approach towards non-dualism. Śaṅkara's is an objective idealism whereas Ramana's is a subjective idealism. Śaṅkara tried to establish the supremacy and sole existence of Brahman, whereas Ramana emphasised that the

'Brahman exists as I'. There is a subtle difference between the two. For Ramana, reality cannot be referred to in the second or third person. Unless we have the first person pronoun I, we cannot have the second and third person, which, in turn, are dependent on the first person pronoun. For Ramana, this first person pronoun I is the only reality that exists.

Aurobindo

Aurobindo's entire teaching recognized the individual self. Although he regarded Brahman as the highest principle, he places relatively more emphasis on manifestations of Brahman. According to Aurobindo, Brahman is involved in matter. Brahman is expressed in matter in increasing degrees. These categories are that of matter, life and mind (in classical Advaita terminology, *anna*, *prāṇa* and *manas*). Here, Matter has only the quality of Existence (*sat*), whereas Life and, especially, Mind also display various grades of the quality of Consciousness (*cit*). In this position, rather than merging oneself in Brahman through Yoga or some other discipline, Aurobindo suggests a conscious attempt to enable an emergence in this world of an even higher manifestation of Brahman, which he calls Supermind, and a corresponding transformation of beings to a diviner race functioning with this principle as a basis.

Again, one can see Aurobindo, at one level, accepting the supremacy of Brahman, but also emphasising the importance given to individuals and their role in the furtherance of evolution. The individual self, too, thus finds its place in his theory.

What we see in Aurobindo's conception of individual self is the use of the concept of degree rather than category. Which means, instead of calling the individual pure Brahman or just matter, Aurobindo says that each individual has a degree of the *Divine* element present in it. And as this element expresses itself more and more, so will humanity evolve. Aurobindo's explanation for the genesis of individuality and individual differences can be attributed to his deterministic stance on the general process of involution and evolution. Humans are mere entities subject to these forces. Such broad claims which refer to humanity as a collective need broad evidence. Such evidence is seldom available to one's empirical self. Thus, this part of Aurobindo's theory is hard to prove or disprove, thereby making it less assessable to scrutiny.

Krishnamurti

Krishnamurti questioned the nature of self. To him, the self was made up of thoughts which, in turn, feed into memory, and this movement of thought in time is self. The quest to transcend the self and thus transcend time, to embark upon the eternal, was the truth that he pointed out in his teachings. But while pointing towards this timeless state, he did recognize physical time. Krishnamurti, in all his teachings, always made a distinction between physical self and psychological self – it was the psychological self that his teachings were concerned with. He often questioned whether time played any role in the transcendence of humans. But he always made it clear that he was not talking about physical chronological time, but psychological time, and, as he clarified that time and memory are needed for the outer world and day-to-day living, in spiritual life, they had no place. Thus, he rejected the notion that knowledge based on memory or continuation of any method or practice in time will help humans attain the transcendental state. Once again, we see that his discourse, too, needs to be understood in the right context and reality and that the self can be understood at different levels.

Krishnamurti refuses to talk about the metaphysical level, criticising it as mere speculation which people indulge in to create a wish-fulfilling dream which makes people feel secure about the continuity of their existence. Krishnamurti speaks about the empirical self and points out that there is no possibility of the existence of such self without the thinking mind. In the thoughtless state of pure observation, he says there is no self. Thus, one can infer that, at a metaphysical level, there is no self. Yet, there is no denial of the empirical self. In fact, he emphasises that the empirical self needs to be fully understood and, in understanding this, there is a possibility of transcending it. Thus, in summary, Krishnamurti recognises the empirical self but does not think that that is the ultimate reality of self. However, he does not talk about the metaphysical level, whether at that level the self exists or not, and, if so, in what way it is experienced.

As we see in the above paragraphs, all the thinkers have mentioned different perspectives in which reality and self can be perceived. Śaṅkara and Ramana downplay the importance of the empirical self, calling it a result of delusion. They uphold the sole existence of the metaphysical self alone. Buddha and Krishnamurti describe this empirical self as a mere cluster. Buddha expressly denies any metaphysical self, whereas Krishnamurti does not comment on it. Aurobindo sees the empirical self as a result of the involution of Brahman and claims that an evolutionary process will take it on further to the greater Divine state. Thus, more than as category, he sees the self as a process. Mahāvīra gives equal importance to both empirical and metaphysical self.

What is common to all these thinkers is that they speak about the mutation and transcendence of the empirical self.

Before we discuss the paths towards self-realisation emerging from each of these thinkers, the subsequent sections describe the hierarchical models of these thinkers elaborating various states of consciousness.

Chapter 12

States and Contents of the Self and Consciousness

In the following sections, different aspects or states of self or consciousness arranged hierarchically are discussed.

Śaṅkara

Śaṅkara's grand guru Gaudapāda, in his commentary on Māṇḍūkya Upaniśad, discusses the following four states of consciousness. Śaṅkara absorbed them from Gaudapāda. Ramana, too, spoke of these. The following is the description of them as it appears in Ramana's teachings.

Jāgrat is the waking state. In it, the *jīva* is the *Visva* aspect and the Lord is the *Virāt* aspect.

Svapna is the dream state in which the *jīva* in the *Taijasa* aspect experiences through the mind the results of the impressions collected in the waking state. All the principles, the five gross elements, the will and the intellect, seventeen in all, together form the subtle body of the dream.

Suṣupti is the state of deep sleep in which the *jīva* in the *Prājñā* aspect experiences the bliss of the Supreme by means of the subtle *avidyā* (nescience). The subtle individual being, after finishing the experiences of the *jāgrat* and *svapna* for the time being, enters with the impressions gathered during those states into the causal body which is made up of nescience.

Turiyā: If, in the *jāgrat* state, the mental activities are stilled and Brahman alone is contemplated, the state is called the *turiyā*. A self-realised individual is said to be residing in *turiyā*.

Humans have all the three states of *jāgrat, svapna* and *sushupti,* which alternate involuntarily. The last state (*turiyā*) is achieved through practise and is the means to liberation. Such realised Self is the light of *Sat, Cit, Ānanda.*

Buddha

In the Patthana section of Abhidhamma, we find a description of the four realities. A thorough understanding of each is needed to liberate oneself from suffering. These realities are: *citta, cetasika, rūpa and nirvāṇa.* Of these, *citta* and *cetasika* exist together. All, except *nirvāṇa,* are *saṁskāradharmas,* i.e., conditioned *dharmas.*

Citta: Loosely defined as consciousness, it can be called the screen on which various mental factors (*cetasika*) arise. There are 121 types of *citta* - twelve immoral, thirty-seven moral, fifty-two resultant, and twenty inoperative. We will also see that the classification of *citta* forms a hierarchy, from '*kāmāva-cara*' to '*lokottara*'.

Cetasika: these are mental factors. There are 50 of them (7 common to all, 14 immoral and 25 moral).

The seven common factors:

- Contact (*phassa*)
- Feeling (*vedanā*)
- Perception (*saññā*)
- Volition (*cetanā*)
- One-pointedness (*ekaggatā*)
- Life faculty (*jīvitindriya*)
- Attention (*manasikāra*)

Rūpa (material form): this is a Buddhist concept for material form. Rūpa can be understood in 3 frameworks:

- *rūpa-khandha* – 'material forms', a category of phenomena.
- *rūpa-āyatana* – 'visible objects', the external sense objects of the eye, by which the world is known
- *nāma-rūpa* – 'name and form', these arise from consciousness and lead to the arising of the sense bases.

Rūpa exists in Rūpa loka and Kāmāloka

Nirvāṇa

Nirvāṇa is the plane where there is no suffering. *Nirvāṇa* being beyond all moral and immoral limitations, has no divisions. It is always present. It exists in the *lokuttara* plane.

Thus, we can see that there are four distinct planes of reality. As will be evident in the next section, these also indicate a journey from gross to subtle, which is the path recommended by Buddha. To elaborate this further, one can look at the further division in the types of *citta*. In all, there are four types of *citta*:

Kāmāvacara – citta

Kāmāvacara citta is the most gross form of consciousness. It dwells in the realm of desire for worldly things. It is fickle, fluctuating and continuously moves around the desires, forming attachments. These attachments are the primary source of suffering.

Rūpāvacara-citta

The consciousness which is unsteady and fluctuating, as in the case of *Kāmāvacara citta,* when slowly starts becoming steady and stable, by way of focusing on some gross material object (i.e., *Rūpa – Rūpa* means matter which has form, colour, etc.), such concentrated consciousness is the *Rūpavacara citta.* Thus, it can be seen that *Rūpavicara* is a *dhyāna* consciousness which is higher than the *Kāmāvacara citta.*

Arūpāvacara citta

Subtler than the *rūpāvacara citta* is *arūpāvacaracitta.* Here the *dhyāna* is on *arūpa,* i.e., the formless. Only with training and practice can a meditator achieve concentration on the formless. As one can see, these are gradual *cittas,* moving from gross to subtle.

Lokottara citta

Loka is the plane of repeated existence. *Lokottara citta* is beyond such a plane. Moving from *rūpāvacara* and *arūpāvacara* when the consciousness is purified and is still without great cravings, the meditator is said to be in the *Lokottara bhūmi* – a plane of tranquillity. This is a much more subtle consciousness compared to the ones mentioned above. It is not fully free, though, of all the subtle impurities at this stage.

Once all these subtle impurities are also removed, then there is the state of *nirvāṇa*. *Nirvāṇa* is attained as a result of taking the consciousness from the gross to subtle and most subtle planes as described in the descriptions above.

Overall, the above details signify that Buddha's teachings illustrate a great deal of elaboration of different mental processes. Consciousness and Cognition can be seen as the most important umbrella terms which explain the various sub-processes of Sensation, Perception, Intentionality and Attention. A great deal of attention has been given to the various processes of mind and the elements which cause the illusion of continuity and permanence.

Mahāvīra

The Jainas explained primarily four types of mental processes called *dhyānas*. Here, the term *dhyāna* means engagement of the mind in a particular thought. These four categories cover all the conditions of mind. The first two cause the ignorance and the other two lead towards the light of liberation.

Ārta-dhyāna, melancholy

Iṣṭa-viyoga, thinking of something pleasant one has lost.

Aniṣṭa-saṁyoga, thinking of something unpleasant one has experienced.

Roga-cintā, thinking of illness.

Nidānārtha, thinking of the future, particularly of the wishes which should be realised in a later existence.

Raudra-dhyāna: mind directed towards cruel, harsh worldly goals, viz. murder, lying, theft and preserving goods.

Hiṁsānandi Raudra dhyāna means thinking delightfully about killing, crushing or destroying living beings either by oneself or through others.

Mṛṣānandi Raudra dhyāna means thinking delightfully about lying, composing deceptive literature, and collecting wealth by deceptive means.

Cauryānandi Raudra dhyāna means thinking delightfully about the act of theft and also preaching dexterity in theft.

Viśayānandi Raudra dhyāna means thinking delightfully about satisfying desires, including being possessive and thinking of fighting ferociously to attain the objects of enjoyment.

Dharma-dhyāna, meditation on the nature of truth and reality.

Ajña-vicaya Dharma dhyāna: Meditating on the flawless and reliable nature of the views expressed by enlightened souls.

Apāya-vicaya Dharma dhyāna: Meditating on how the true character of the self is clouded by its contact with *kasayas* such as anger, pride, etc.

Vipāka-vicaya Dharma dhyāna: Meditating on the nature of the results of various karmas.

Loka-samsthāna-vicaya Dharma Dhyāna: Meditating on the nature of the universe (*Loka*).

Śukla-dhyāna, pure meditation.

Pṛthaktva-vitarka is directed towards conduct and the contradictions in the process of the world.

Ekatva- vitarka is directed towards the soul as the one which sustains all changes.

Sūkṣma-kriyā-pratipatti is directed towards suppressing the activity which still exists to a minimal degree.

Uparata- kriyānivrtti is focussed on complete liberation from *karmas*.

Ramana

As stated in the section on Śaṅkara's conception of various states of consciousness, we noted that Ramana provided a similar description. However, apart from the four states of *jagrat, svapna, suṣupti* and *turiya*, Ramana mentions another fifth state called *turiyātita*.

Ramana only occasionally uses the term *turiyātita*. Most of the time, he mentions the four states similar to the traditional view. In fact, he explains that *turiya* is actually not a separate fourth state, but that which underlies all three states of *jāgrat, svapna and suṣupti*. For sake of understanding, he says that, the fourth separate state is mentioned.

Similarly, one may ask then why mention another fifth state? The answer to this too seems to be more for convenience of explanation rather than positing an actual separate state. This can be seen clearly in the following response of Ramana in his book Spiritual Instruction:

> *Turiya* means that which is the fourth. The experiencers (*jīvas*) of the three states of waking, dreaming and deep sleep, known as *vishva, taijasa* and *prajna*, who wander successively in

these three states, are not the Self. It is with the object of making this clear, namely that the Self is that which is different from them and which is the witness of these states, that it is called the fourth (*turiya*). When this is known, the three experiencers disappear and the idea that the Self is a witness, that it is the fourth, also disappears. That is why the Self is described as beyond the fourth (*turiyatita*)."

Aurobindo

Similarly, in Aurobindo's philosophy too, we find different levels of existence, namely, the physical, vital, mental and psychic. Consciousness gradually rises from physical to psychic.

Krishnamurti

On similar lines to Buddha, Krishnamurti, in his teachings, focussed greatly on the everyday experiences of human beings, of fear, sorrow, ambition, conflict and violence. It is the true understanding of these phenomena which, according to him, would free human beings from the trap of mind and time.

When it comes to self, as can be seen, in all the above thinkers' theories, a great deal of attention has been paid to the states and contents of consciousness. Invariably, there are descriptions of various states, levels and types of mental processes.

It is these mental models and mental process that the individual has to tread and pass through to attain what is truly the nature of Self, whether permanent or non-existent and empty, but the truth has to be discovered through the seemingly common categories of mind and consciousness.

It may be noted that the very way of looking at different mental models in the case of each thinker resonates very strongly with the particular metaphysical positions that they take. The advaitins want to prove and establish the permanent Brahman in which nothing changes and it remains the eternal indivisible sole existent absolute principle. Thus, we can see that Śaṅkara's theory does not elaborate much beyond the states of consciousness.

Whereas, on the other hand, as Buddha has to emphasise the impermanent, clustered nature of mind and matter, the various factors and processes of mind have been emphasized showing how these fragments then create the illusion of a permanent self.

Mahāvīra's essential teaching of purification of the soul from karma naturally talks of mental processes that either attract more karmas or help in getting rid of them.

With a thinker like Aurobindo, whose theory's primary objective is the evolution of consciousness from matter to energy, one can see the emphasis on describing various levels and the encouragement given to move to higher and higher levels of consciousness.

In the case of Krishnamurti, whose teachings were directed against establishing or believing any theory, he simply left aside anything and everything that is not directly relevant to human experience. Thus, he talks about relationships, comparison, jealousy, authority and, amidst these experiences, suggests discovering the self.

Chapter 13

The Roles of God, Guru and Karma

The thinkers discussed here were not just philosophers, they were teachers and had a definite purpose in revealing to others the true nature of self and to facilitate people's realisation of the truth and the self. All these thinkers discussed in previous chapters revealed their philosophy through their public discourses or dialogues and question and answer sessions with seekers, except for Śaṅkara and Aurobindo, who wrote extensively several philosophical texts and commentaries. Thus, the question of self-realisation is not a merely academic or philosophical one, but something these thinkers urged everyone to practice and attain, which they described as the highest. In this section, we will discuss comparatively the roles of God, Guru and Karma in self-realisation.

God

What is the role of God in an individual's self-realisation? The popular view of God as a creator and regulator of the world and of humans is absent in all the theories discussed here. Śaṅkara and Aurobindo do talk about the concept of *Īśvara* or the Divine, but this God is not separate from us or the world but is the very Brahman. Thus, we can conveniently put aside the notion of the God as an agent in self-realisation. This could be a significant uniting commonality in various views discussed here. When God is kept out of the most important endeavour of self-realisation, it is the self with its efforts which becomes the primary focus. A great deal of emphasis is given on the self in all these traditions. Whereas in the West, such emphasis has been evident only in the last few centuries, especially after the 'Age of Enlightenment', when strong theistic religious views were opposed to make room for an enquiry about the self.

Guru

If not God, the second most important entity in the Indian spiritual systems can be the Guru. In Śaṅkara's system, a guru is essential for an individual to attain self-realisation. What is then the role of the Guru? According to Śaṅkara, the Guru uses words in such a way so as to awaken the understanding in the disciple of the true meaning of Vedānta and other texts as part of the *Śruti*.

The fact that a Guru is indispensable is expressed clearly in the following verses by Śaṅkara:

> Even if, as in accordance with the Vedic passages proclaiming identity, the self is revealed without any interruption, it is

impossible to realise it without the grace of a Guru. Do not think as to what is the need for a Guru, as one can attain self-realisation by avoiding prohibited rotes and by purifying the mind by performing the prescribed rites by oneself. Self-realisation cannot result from rites alone, without the Guru, who is an ocean of mercy. The Vedas have established that only the one who has a Guru can attain (self) knowledge. (Svātmanirūpaṇa: 41-43)

Such a Guru must have the following qualities

Śrotriya - must be learned in the Vedic scriptures and *sampradāya*

Brahmaniṣṭha - meaning literally 'established in Brahman'; must have realised the oneness of Brahman in everything and in himself

As mentioned earlier, the guru-disciple system has a great importance in the Śaṅkara's system. Upon fulfilling the four requisites (*Sādhana Chatuṣṭaya;* elaborated in the next section), knowledge of the Brahman is acquired only after initiation into the *Śrutis.* This initiation into understanding the meaning of *Śrutis*, which reveal the nature of Brahman, cannot happen without having a guru. Thus, although one can infer that for ultimate self-realisation, the Vedas and the Guru need to be transcended, the role of a Guru is crucial in Śaṅkara's system.

All the other thinkers may not give equal importance to a guru. Śaṅkara himself had a guru from whom he learnt, whereas all the other thinkers discovered the truth by their own efforts, independent of any guru. Mahāvīra and Buddha did recognize the role of a teacher, and played it too, but their concept of a teacher is different from that of Śaṅkara's. Śaṅkara bases his theories on the Vedas and Upaniṣads, and a great many discourses are available in the Vedas on the guru-disciple relationship, which transforms the role of the guru from a mere teacher to someone who can actually bring about realisation in the disciple. In the *śramaṇa* traditions of Buddha and Mahāvīra, a teacher is a person who is ahead on the path – the same path that the disciple is on, the path as shown by the enlightened ones.

One person to actively speak against Gurudom was Krishnamurti. Krishnamurti questioned every kind of authority and said that we seek any authority merely to continue the self which is ever seeking security, as an escape from the problems of daily living, the problems of fear, jealousy, and conflict and so on. For him, any acceptance of a system or a guru fragmented our perception, as whatever the self chooses is a result of past conditioning which furthers the conditioning and the sense of separate 'I', thus choosing a guru or following a guru as an authority is to already create barrier to understanding the truth –the truth which, as he perceived, is ever new and cannot be captured by old mind which chooses based on past knowledge.

Thus, in this regard, both Śaṅkara and Ramana believe in a Guru's capacity to enlighten the disciple. Aurobindo encourages individuals to seek inner guidance and also seek the grace of divine, whereas Buddha, Mahāvīra and Krishnamurti can be seen as teachers emphasising individual efforts.

Some grave risks attached to gurudom are evident. Not every person who claims to be a guru is eligible to be so. A seeker, because s/he is ignorant, may not be in a position to assess the guru. Secondly, the capacity of a guru to bring about realisation in a disciple is debatable. If such a capacity exists, one may question as to why the guru will not use it uniformly for everyone? What is the place of individual practice in such scenario? Another most common problem with the notion of a guru is that it becomes most commonly associated with power. Power in turn leads to corruption. Due to such multiple issues related to the issue of the guru-disciple relationship, the indispensable position of a guru can be strongly challenged.

There is certainly a great value in one person benefitting from another person's guidance. Teachers such as Buddha not only recognised its importance but put it on a very high pedestal. The concept of *kalyāṇa-mitratā*or spiritual friendship as taught by the Buddha signifies this. Such friendship is primarily between the student and teacher. It can also be between peers. On various occasions, Buddha stated that such a relationship was the best way to progress on the spiritual path. The spirit of this relationship is different to that advocated by Śaṅkara. Buddha encourages this relationship for the motivation and support to progress on the spiritual path. However, the real progress happens as a result of individual striving.

Karma and Ethics

Although the act of self-realisation is approached initially through the mental process of meditation, (which later transcends the mental), several other factors, though not directly causing self-realisation, are considered as being supportive of this. They can be broadly addressed by analysing the principle of karma, with ethics as its subset.

If realisation and knowledge, as symbolized by Light in the Vedas and many other systems, is at one end of the spectrum, then its opposite force, the element of *Avidyā*, the ignorance symbolized by darkness, is at its other end. This concept of *avidyā* needs due attention in the discourse on self-realisation. The processes causing *avidyā* or *mithyātva* (as in Jain philosophy), can be well explained by the psychological tendencies or *kaṣāyas* leading to the bondage of karma. Both Buddha and Mahāvīra recognize the effect of good and bad karma and their role in self-realisation. Śaṅkara and Ramana, however, restrict their elaborations on the whole issue of *prārabdha*, again owing to their view that, ultimately, *avidyā* is unreal and in the case of Ramana, his view that everything is predestined.

Chapter 14

The Way to Self-realisation (Sādhanā)

Prerequisites for Sādhanā

By eliminating God and minimizing the role of the guru to an instructor or a guide, if not fully eliminating it, a great deal of responsibility for self-realisation can come to the individual herself. In this chapter, we shall look at the key practices leading to self-realisation, as emerging from the different systems and theories discussed so far.

Before that, here is a brief account of certain prerequisites for *Sādhanā* as stated by these thinkers.

According to Śaṅkara, these prerequisites are as follows:

Sādhana Chatuṣṭaya

Something therefore needs to be said about the conditions to be fulfilled before beginning

> to deliberate on Brahman. They are i) discrimination between the eternal and the non-eternal ii) dispassion regarding the enjoyment of the result of present and future deeds iii) perfection of such practices as control of the mind, control of the sense organs, etc., and (iv) desire to attain *Mokṣa*. Granting the existence of these, Brahman can be deliberated upon or known even before or after the enquiry into *Dharma*, but not otherwise. Therefore, with the word *'atha'*, is enjoined the succession to a perfection of the practices mentioned here. (Brahma sūtra Śaṅkarabhāsya 1-1-1-1)

To describe in detail any *mumukṣu* (one seeking *mokṣa*) has to have the following four *Sampattis* (qualifications), collectively called *Sādhana Chatuṣṭaya Sampatti* ("the fourfold qualifications"):

Nityānitya-vastu Viveka — The ability to correctly discriminate between eternal (*nitya*) and transitory existence (*anitya*).

Ihāmutrārtha-phala-bhoga-virāga The renunciation (*virāga*) of the enjoyment of objects (*artha-phala-bhoga*) in this world (*iha*) and the other worlds (*amutra*), such as heaven, etc.

Śamādi-ṣaṭka-sampatti— the sixfold qualities,

Śama (control of the *antaḥkaraṇa*).

Dama (control of external sense organs).

Uparati (cessation of these external organs so restrained from the pursuit of objects, or it may mean the abandonment of the prescribed works according to scriptural injunctions).

Titikṣā (toleration of *tāpatraya*).

Śraddhā (faith in Guru and the Vedas).

Samādhāna (concentrating of the mind on God and Guru).

Mumukṣutva - The firm conviction that the nature of the world is misery and the intense longing for mokṣa (release from the cycle of births and deaths).

Śaṅkara states in Tattva bodha (1.2) that *mokṣa* is available only to those possessing the above-mentioned fourfold qualifications. Thus, any seeker wishing to study Advaita Vedānta from a teacher must possess these qualifications.

In the case of Mahāvīra, *samyak darśan* is said to be the starting point of *Sādhanā*. It is interpreted as right faith. There are certain fundamental principles in Mahāvīra's teachings. Unless an individual has basic faith in these principles, s/he would not be able to take the necessary steps in progressing on the spiritual path.

Buddha gave such primary importance to practising *Śila*. *Śila* provides the foundation for *samādhi* and *prajñā*.

As we will see in the next section, the modern thinkers took a more direct approach to *Sādhanā*. None of them demanded faith in scriptures or the necessity of a guru. They encouraged individuals to plunge into direct experience of their selves and to realise their true nature. Perhaps the approach of the ancient thinkers too may have been simpler and more direct compared to how it appears today. Often, when the pioneer passes away, the interpreters assume positions of power and may influence the interpretations according to their own understanding and preferences. Centuries of such interpretations and philosophisation of their teachings may have added to the complexities of their teachings, or, at least, have created such an impression.

Techniques of Sādhanā

There are various techniques and methods that these thinkers have suggested which appear in the body of work produced by them in their lifetime. Here, we shall consider the most important hallmark ways from each system and analyse the underlying principles so as to arrive at a unified understanding of the way to self-realisation.

As discussed in the earlier section, Śaṅkara suggests that upon meditating on the true meaning of Brahman, one can attain the knowledge of Brahman and that understanding will liberate the individual. There is no elaborate description given as to the phenomenon of self-realisation in his work. Aurobindo too does not have a specific method, but recommends that making the mind quiet will liberate it, as, in the quiet mind, the truth of Brahman can appear directly. This is very different from the teachings of Buddha and Mahāvīra, where a great deal of importance and description is given of the practices which will eventually purify the person and take him/her to the path of liberation or *mokṣa* or *nirvāṇa*.

For Buddha, the most important realisation that an individual can have, which will free him from the sorrow, was that of *anitya* – impermanence, and this realisation leading to the realisation of *anātman* – absence of any permanent self or atman. If one meditates and observes the physical and mental processes, one can see that everything is always changing. *Vipassana* is one of the meditation techniques proposed by Buddhism which helps an individual to attain *nirvāṇa* by awakening the individual's *prajñā*.

In Mahāvīra's teachings, the seven principles explained in previous chapters hold the key to self-realisation. Jīva, the self upon incurring present karma and already bound by the past karma, feels the bondage. It is by *Saṁvara* that the *āshrava* is blocked and that is the point from where the *nirjarā* can ultimately begin to lead to *Mokṣa*.

The difference between Ramana and Śaṅkara is their approach towards self-realisation. Where Śaṅkara emphasised the importance of studying scriptures, Ramana's single supreme way to awaken and realise the self is through self-enquiry. Throughout his life, he asked people to enquire into 'who am I'. For every thought, every feeling, every question that arises in the person's mind, one can ask the question, 'who is this thought arising to?'. Upon truly meditating on this, one can again go on asking the same question to all the answers that emerge, as to 'who is this answer coming from?'. This ultimately will collapse the dichotomy between the subject and object, and the illusory 'I' will disappear leaving the silence and the sense of Oneness which is not fragmented by the notion of 'I'. The 'I' essentially arises due to sheer mental strivings and not enquiring into the true nature of self.

Krishnamurti placed a great deal of importance on choiceless awareness. The very act of understanding the self involves neither justifying nor condemning any thought or feeling, but being in total contact with the object of perception without naming it. Upon doing so, the subject, the I, too appears as an object and the limited fragment which we regard as the 'I' disappears and this leads to freedom from the image of self which is central to all humans. This happens through a thorough understanding of the processes that create and sustain the self. Of course, he does not use any orthodox term to describe this liberated state, such as Brahman, but often denotes this state as the one of Love, Beauty or Freedom.

In summary, these preceding sections compared the theories in light of the fact that each theory discussed the issue of self as empirical, as well as at a higher level (though sometimes self was denied at a higher level, as in the case of Buddhism). In this light, we saw the concepts of *Pāramārthika* and *Vyavahārikasattā*, the Buddhist *skandhas,* and concepts of physical self and psychological self appearing in Krishnamurti's works are relevant. To prove the same point, the discussion on levels of consciousness was elaborated. The levels of consciousness appearing in Advaita, Jaina and Buddhist philosophies, along with the modern theorists, are described.

Based on the theories of Self, each school advocates specific methods of self-realisation. All such methods were critically compared with reference to role of God, Guru and individual practices *(sādhana).*

We have seen that, though generally no-one has denied self at an empirical level, there are diverse approaches at the level of metaphysical self and also in the methods and techniques prescribed for self-realisation.

In the next chapter, the aim is to arrive at a synthesis of these approaches, building on the discussions so far.

Synthesis

On reading the description of Buddhism, which emphasises the sole existence of the phenomenon of impermanence, and the wholly opposing view proposed by Śaṅkara, which emphasises that nothing but the eternal permanent Brahman exists, one may wonder where the Jain view stands in comparison. Here, the epistemological system of Mahāvīra, which is also the logical framework which Mahāvīra put forth for any philosophical theory viz. Anekāntavāda and the offshoots of it, namely Syādvāda and Nayavāda, must also be considered and consulted. According to Anekāntavāda, language is not capable of affirming any absolute universal truth. The truth is multifold and has many aspects, and it is the function of knowledge and philosophy to be able to decipher or differentiate between the validity of each statement claiming to be true in accordance with or in conjunction with or pertaining to the specific aspect of reality.

Thus, what we are stating here is that Mahāvīra's model of anekāntavāda helps us take an integrated view of reality. In fact, the Jaina doctrine of Anekāntavāda, along with its offshoots viz. Syādvāda and Nayavāda, can be used as a methodological tool to arrive at a synthesis of rival views. So let us give a brief account of the Jaina doctrines and then try to apply this method to the views of the thinkers under consideration.

Chapter 15

Anekāntavāda as a Methodological Tool for Synthesis

When considering and discussing any ideology and also different ideologies together, it is important to have a language which recognises its limitations, and the readership has to have a shared understanding of terms and principles. Especially when the subject is metaphysics, it becomes most important to proceed with care to avoid what can easily be seen as a conceptual chaos or misunderstandings that arise purely as a result of not understanding the meaning behind each view. Jainism makes a unique contribution to developing a synergistic and comprehensive approach applicable to various ideologies and in reducing chaos, misunderstanding and conflict. To understand this better, three key principles need to be understood at the outset:

Anekāntavāda

Anekāntavāda is one of the most important and fundamental doctrines of Jainism. It denotes that truth can be perceived differently from different points of view, and that it cannot be expressed in a single point of view. It states that objects are infinite in their qualities and modes of existence, so they cannot be completely grasped in all their aspects and manifestations by limited human perception, upholding the principle of pluralism. Anekāntavāda is further expressed by Syādvāda 'conditioned viewpoints' and Nayavāda 'partial viewpoints'.

Syādvāda

Syādvāda can be seen as the theory of conditioned predication. Here, it is recommended that every expression be prefixed by *Syād*, meaning "perhaps" or "maybe". Syādvāda ensures that any statement is seen as true only from one perspective. This is to remove the dogmatism from any philosophical claim. This is especially essential as reality is complex and needs a system which can express it more fully. There are seven such different conditional and relative viewpoints or propositions by which a statement can be expressed. This is known as saptibhaṅgīnāya or the theory of seven conditioned predications. These seven propositions, also known as saptibhaṅgī, are:

1. *syād-asti*—in some ways, it is,
2. *syād-nāsti*—in some ways, it is not,
3. *syād-asti-nāsti*—in some ways, it is, and it is not,
4. *syād-asti-avaktavyaḥ*—in some ways, it is, and it is indescribable,

5. *syād-nāsti-avaktavyaḥ*—in some ways, it is not, and it is indescribable,

6. *syād-asti-nāsti-avaktavyaḥ*—in some ways, it is, it is not, and it is indescribable,

7. *syād-avaktavyaḥ*—in some ways, it is indescribable.

Each of these seven propositions examines the complex and multifaceted nature of reality from a relative point of view of time, space, substance and mode.

Nayavāda

Nayavāda is the theory of partial standpoints or viewpoints. It is used to arrive at a certain inference from a point of view. An object has infinite aspects to it, but when we describe an object in practice, we speak only of relevant aspects and ignore irrelevant ones. This does not deny the other attributes, qualities, modes and other aspects. They are merely irrelevant from a particular perspective. This particular viewpoint is called a *naya* or a partial viewpoint. As a type of critical philosophy, Nayavāda holds that all philosophical disputes arise out of the confusion of standpoints, and that the standpoints we adopt are, although we may not realise it, "the outcome of purposes that we may pursue". *Naya*, being a partial expression of truth, enables us to comprehend the reality part by part. It is within these frameworks that the Jain philosophy as given by Mahāvīra is best understood.

Nayas are classified in Jainism in two ways. One well-known classification is sevenfold, where seven *nayas* represent seven partial standpoints and they are philosophically on par with each other. There is no hierarchy among them. However, according to

Jainism, to treat any of the partial standpoints as complete or comprehensive is a fallacy (Nayābhāsa or Durānaya). For instance, Saṅgrahanaya is a partial standpoint which emphasises the 'universal' and neglects particularity. But to overemphasize the universal and deny particularity is a fallacy of *naya*. According to Jainas, Advaita vedantins who regard 'Sattā' (the realness which is the nature of Brahman) as the only reality and deny the reality of particular facts commit Saṅgrahabhāsa.

Similarly, Ṛjusūtranaya is the standpoint which emphasizes the present momentary phenomena and neglects continuity. Overemphasising momentariness and denying continuity would be a fallacy called Ṛjusūtrabhāsa, which is committed by Buddhists, according to Jainas. Jainas, in their Anekānta approach, try to accommodate universals as well particulars, and momentariness as well as continuity.

The other classification of *nayas* is the twofold classification between Niścayanaya and Vyavāharanaya. According to it, Vyavāharanaya is the conventional standpoint, whereas Niścayanaya is the ultimate standpoint. This classification is parallel to the similar classification in Vedānta and Buddhism. In Vedānta, we have Pāramārthika sattā and Vyavāhārika sattā, whereas in Buddhism we have Paramārthatah Satya and Lokasaṁvṛti Satya.

However, when we are using Anekāntavāda - Syādvāda and Nayavāda - as methodological tools for arriving at a synthesis of diverse or rival views, the sevenfold classification of naya is more relevant than the twofold classification between Niścaya and Vyavāhara.

Anekāntavāda, it must be noted, forms part of Mahāvīra's metaphilosophy. Metaphilosophy investigates the methods used by philosophy. Anekāntavāda as a metaphilosophy provides a system of understanding reality in its different aspects without limiting our understanding of certain specific attributes of reality as the whole reality. As elaborated in this chapter, anekāntavāda can be used as a useful tool to arrive at the synthesis of various theories that appear in this work. This metaphilosophical tool, however, should not be mixed with Mahāvīra's philosophy of self and self-realisation. Anekāntavāda is used here as a neutral tool which helps us appreciate the diverse theories by bringing them onto the same platform. It helps seemingly opposite views co-exist as different aspects of reality.

Chapter 16

Synthesis

In summary, it is clear that each thinker included in this work recognizes that reality pertaining to the self can be seen in more than one way. On the metaphysical level, even though these thinkers have diverse views of Self, they recognize that, at the empirical level, the self is felt in different categories. These categories can be different states of consciousness which affect how the self and reality are perceived, or these can be different mental processes which create certain effects in the consciousness and the content of consciousness. Invariably, the fragments of such mental divisions and processes create the self as commonly felt by individuals. Such self is also bound by *duḥkha* (suffering) and bondage and, at a more empirical level, with the emotions of fear, anger, conflict, and so on. Such self is always transient and limited by its conditioning.

What these thinkers also point towards is a possibility of transcending this limited self towards something that is eternally freeing and pure – an ideal often captured in the term 'self-realisation'.

When it comes to various approaches and methods of self-realisation according to the selected thinkers discussed above, one can note that all the thinkers studied here rely predominantly on knowledge as the path. Knowledge which is direct and experiential. The knowledge that The self as we normally identify it is centred on the body and senses, and consequently, also on the resulting pleasures and pains that we experience. Such understanding of limitedness, finiteness can be the first stage. This includes understanding what we call the mind, with all its attractions and aversions. This self is of transient nature, resulting in lives which are not free, but instead are bound by craving for pleasure and aversion to pain. The essential nature of the self is far different to what is normally experienced in such a manner. The self can realise its ideal state, which is markedly different from what is described above. Such a realised state as described by the states of *nirvāṇa* or *mokṣa* is essentially where freedom from limitation is experienced. Śaṅkara describes this state as *sat-cidānanda*, the blissful consciousness devoid of any sorrow, fear or confusion. Once the body of such a realised individual dies, the final limitations of the body are overcome, too.

The way to realise this is often summarised as the practice of 'meditation' in almost all the schools studied here. In Śaṅkara's teachings, meditation is predominantly contemplation of the nature of reality as Brahman, to see that everything is Brahman and also to see finally the very self as Brahman. Buddhist meditations focus on the opposite principle. Instead of asserting and believing in the principle of Brahman as endorsed by the

Upaniṣads, Buddha advised observing the very nature of things as impermanent. As the observing becomes subtler, the impermanence is seen more and more clearly, including the impermanence of the self, finally creating a way to realise that there is no self. Thus, when one is freed from the limitation of the self and all the striving that arise from the self, a state of *nirvāṇa* is achieved. Mahāvīra's practical teachings are in a certain harmony with the above currents, inasmuch as they disagree with the philosophical assertions which Śaṅkara and Buddha adhere to. The problems arising out of denial of self (which both Śaṅkara and Buddha do by asserting a permanent and impermanent reality) are done away with in Mahāvīra's philosophy, where, on a practical level, he accepts the existence of an individual entity and, by practices of knowledge, conduct and meditation, one realises the transient nature of the non-living principle and eventually the infinite permanence of the unbound soul best described by the abstract term *'kevala jñāna'* – literally 'only knowledge', or 'pure knowing'.

The philosophical views of Śaṅkara, Buddha and Mahāvīra seem to highlight different aspects of reality – viz. Śaṅkara: the non-changing aspect of reality – Brahman, Buddha: the impermanent aspect of reality and absence of a permanent self, and Mahāvīra: the co-existence of finite and infinite aspects of reality. However, in essence, all the thinkers point to the application of right knowledge accompanied by right conduct, leading to a realisation of true self, which simultaneously opens the door to realising the nature of the universe. Mahāvīra's words, *"Appā so paramappā"*, i.e., "the soul is God", and Śaṅkara's words: *"Aham Brahmāsmi"*, "I am God or the eternal principal", all symbolise the path and its destination of a free state in which the joyful consciousness is in constant touch with the truth – both personal and universal (although this distinction does not exist for the realised soul).

One can see that when it comes to actually applying the various metaphysical principles of these theories to practical empirical criteria, one has to take into account the various explanations which are given as additional concepts of the same theory. These details allow a broader explanation, which is more holistic, rather than a one-sided principle which often creates more debate and dispute with seemingly opposite theories. However, when the same theories are seen in a multi-faceted manner, the scope to decipher certain common elements present in different theories can exist, thus making it possible to advance one's understanding of the subject matter without having to prove and disprove certain one-sided viewpoints. It is on such parameters that we will base our further discussion.

The question of self can be addressed at two levels: the ideal and the conventional, i.e., the metaphysical and the empirical. Whereas both views hold true in their place, it is important to begin at the level of empirical phenomena. Advaitins' claims are often too ideal and seem to deny a great deal of the every-day experience of human beings. The view that everything is Brahman and the self too is nothing but Brahman has a strong appeal to a philosophical mind which is looking for meaning in the rather transient world where nothing seems to last. Brahman, with its sat-cit-ānanda nature, brings that eternal principle to us to aspire to, to recognize that it binds all of existence as one. Upon upholding the Brahman as the sole truth, everything else, unfortunately, has to be swept aside as *Māyā* or illusion. This, although it may be fair to not let Brahman dilute its charisma, cannot suffice when a Buddha stands and says that *duḥkha* is an *āryasatya*. The fact of sorrow and the suffering of old age and death and disease may seem more real than the idea of Brahman.

The *śramaṇaic* systems of Mahāvīra and Buddha have always urged each human being to work (as the term *śrama* denotes) towards his/her enlightenment, whereas we find Śaṅkara asking us to mediate upon the nature of Brahman and 'see' that everything is one.

Śaṅkara's *Mokṣa* does find a great deal of resonance with Mahāvīra's *Kaivalya* and Buddha's *Nirvāṇa*. However, one can note that the *Śramaṇaic* systems have gone to greater lengths in elaborating the path, which not only include the meditative practices but elaborately explain the karma principle and weave it through the ethics and the metaphysics. A heavy emphasis on ethics does seem to be somewhat lacking in Śaṅkara's teachings. When it comes to the karma theory, the Jain systems of karmic *pudgala*, though seemingly rather imaginary, do provide a basis of explaining the ideal and the apparent reality in their classic Anekāntavāda model.

The synthesis based on this common core of these thinkers is elaborated in the following. The differences in the metaphysical positions held by these thinkers, and the consequent differences in the techniques of self-realisation proposed by them, can be accounted for by their temperamental differences. Each thinker can be seen as emphasizing certain aspects of reality. Such differences can be not only considered permissible but appreciated, provided that one-sided rigidity and absolutism of any kind is avoided. This can be done well in the spirit of Anekāntavāda.

(Anekāntavāda, in our day, is also known as academic non-violence.)

The soul or the *jīva* in its purest state, as explained by Mahāvīra has qualities of permanence and infinite joy, power, knowledge, which is very similar to the attributes of Brahman. At the same time, the constantly changing karmic body made of *pudgalas*, and, in the case of Buddha, of what he called *saṅghata*, are in constant flux. It was this aspect of reality and self that Buddha emphasised. For Mahāvīra, both these truths, or realities, co-exist and are not mutually exclusive. The *syādvāda* reminds us to consider any absolute statement, viz. 'everything is impermanent' or 'everything is permanent', with greater curiosity and to ask, is reality only this? Or, in the way *syādvāda* principles suggest, reality is also this, as in 'everything is impermanent, and everything is also permanent.' The critical question here would be what aspect of reality we are focusing on when we make these statements. It is this broad sense of understanding that Mahāvīra propagated. Thus, the Jain system would have no problem in accepting Śaṅkara's notion and the Buddhist notion in the same breath by simply asserting that both these principles speak different aspects of the one universal reality often impossible to explain in language, it being, however, possible to appreciate it better by the use of Anekāntavāda, as explained earlier.

When it comes to the path of self-realisation, apart from the various views discussed in previous chapters, one notices that the methods of self-realisation are supported by various aspects of conduct. Whether it is *Śila, Samādhi* and *Prajñā* of Buddha, or *Samyak Jñāna, Samyak Darśana and Samyak Caritra* of Mahāvīra, we see that a person's intentions, actions and speech all account for a life leading to self-realisation. Of speech, action and thought, it is thought which is given the most importance. The constant psychological process of *Rāga* and *Dveśa* also implied by *Ārtadhyāna* and *Raudra dhyāna* are the primary cause of attracting new karmas which prevent the individual from realizing his/her true self. Unless the mind is quietened by transcending the mental striving for gaining pleasure and avoiding pain, it is not possible to transcend the limited self, to realise the Self that one is. This particular point is common to all the thinkers. In Krishnamurti's words,

> We must first be cognizant of our own ideals, pursuits, wants, without accepting or condemning them as being right or wrong. At present, we cannot discern what is true and what is false, what is lasting and what is transient, because the mind is so crippled with its own self-created wants, ideals and escapes that it is incapable of true perception."

Samādhi, śukla dhyāna, mindful *prajñā* that these thinkers indicate demand such choiceless awareness in thought, speech and action. The notion of *ahiṁsā* thus goes beyond the non-killing, *ahiṁsā,* as a way of life denotes a life of full awareness (*yatanā*) which ensures no other being is violated as a result of personal selfishness. Awareness, thus, is the single point which can be considered as the key that each of these thinkers is emphasizing. It is this *samatā,* the equanimity as practiced in Buddhist *Vipassanā* or Jain practice of *Sāmayik* that brings about the balance and the peace in which the ultimate reality of the self and the universe - as indicated by the term Brahman by Śaṅkara or Buddha's eternal happiness or Mahāvīra's *Keval Jñāna*, the pure awareness and the resultant omniscience - is realised.

The result of self-realisation is described by the enlightened ones as *Satchidananda, Nirvāṇa, Mokṣa* or *Kaivalya*. Again, the *Sat* aspect can be seen as emphasising the positive presence of *Ānanda*, whereas *Nir-vāna* might emphasize the absence of *Duḥkha*, although Buddha too uses the word *'paramam sukham'*, i.e., 'the ultimate bliss' to describe the state of *Nirvāṇa*.

Summary

As stated initially, the purpose of this work was not to look at the metaphysical aspects of the theories of selected key thinkers from ancient and modern India. The thrust was to understand the key components of ways of looking at theories of self and the methods of self-realisation. With a brief reference to the Western theories of self which gained importance in the Enlightenment period, the entire body of this work focused on the selected Indian thinkers.

Previous chapters included, along with a description of each thinker's viewpoints, a critical look at the problems posed by each view and the implications for the theories of self and practices of self-realisation. What is presented in this chapter are the key observations which appear in a scattered way all across this book, but presented here as a synthesis of specific ancient and modern Indian thought.

It must be admitted that the Anekāntavāda, with its forms of Nayavāda and Syādvāda, provides us a great opportunity to appreciate Śaṅkara's permanent Brahman, and at the same time, Buddha's *anātman* and *anitya*, by allowing the reality to be complex and multi-layered, while seemingly contradictory principles can not only coexist but complement each other and bring out the aspect of reality which may be lacking in one limited view. The Jain theory does bring Śaṅkara and Buddha together.

There is a clear advantage that we have in studying the modern thinkers, since the language they used is contemporary and clear accounts of their theories are available to us. Ramana and Krishnamurti clearly focused on the transformation of man, whereas Aurobindo treated the mission of transformation to a vast extent, in which he called his Yoga an instrument in advancing the evolution of mankind into the next *supramental* species. Whether individual or collective, a single point emphasized by all the thinkers, modern and ancient was the cultivation of awareness as the single most important avenue for self-realisation. The foundation of ethical living works in parallel to support spiritual living, and simultaneously, spiritual mindful living enriches and strengthens ethical living.

Working on the mind to make it completely peaceful, devoid of opposite tendencies, as a result, it finally encounters the subject-object dichotomy. Upon diligently enquiring into it, the observer and observed, the knower and known are perceived as either One or none, thus freeing the ego from the shackles of fragmented existence into the vast Oneness or Nothingness. Now whether such a state is described by the terms Brahman, or *Nirvāṇa*, is immaterial as the very proponents of these concepts admit that such a thing (although it is not a thing) is indescribable by words, *acintya, avarnanīya*. Mahāvīra's principle of anekāntavāda too is based on the fact that language is limited and any one statement about reality is incapable of capturing the complete absolute truth.

Thus, in summary, the differences in various thinkers' viewpoints are a result of certain metaphysical positions they chose to assert. The broader frameworks (like that of Anekāntavāda) can bring the different theories together into a more comprehensive and inclusive model. As every thinker accepts reality at different levels, it is the methods of meditation in which the nature of self is enquired, which clearly can break the subject-object dichotomy, so that self-realisation is achieved.

To do this, a great deal of attention needs to be paid to conduct, as the karmic principles are closely linked with self-realisation.

The scriptures can provide the initial support, but it is the individual who needs to inculcate the principles of awareness in his/her life. The extent to which the individual can cleanse his/her mind of several psychological tendencies, and the purification thereby achieved, enables the realisation of the self.

These common principles are in harmony with all the above theories and thus lead to the transcendent states of freedom and oneness, as denoted by the terms *mokṣa, nirvāṇa or kevala jñāna.*

Bibliography

Aiyar, Ramachandra C.V. (1988). *Sri Sankara's Gita Bhashya.* Bombay : Bharatiya Vidya Bhavan.

Aristotle, R. D. H. (2008). *De Anima.* New York: Cosimo.

Atkins, K. (2000). "Autonomy and the subjective character of experience". *Journal of Applied Philosophy 17:1.*

Aurobindo, Sri (1992). *The Synthesis of Yoga.* Pondycherry: Lotus Press.

Aurobindo, Sri (1993). *The Integral Yoga: Sri Aurobindo's Teaching and Method of Practice.* Pondycherry: Lotus Press.

Aurobindo, Sri (1997). *Complete Works of Sri Aurobindo.* Pondycherry: Sri Aurobindo Ashram.

Bhagavat, Hari Raghunath (Ed.) (1927). *The Upaniṣadbhashya.* Pune: Ashtekar & Co.

Bhattacharyya, Haridas (2006). *The Cultural Heritage of India.* Kolkota: The Ramakrishna Mission Institute of Culture.

Bodhi, B. (1999). *A comprehensive manual of Abhidhamma: the Abhidhammattha sangaha of Ācariya Anuruddha.* Kandy: Buddhist Publication Society.

Carriero, J. P. (2009). Between two worlds: a reading of Descartes's Meditations. Woodstock: Princeton University Press.

Chatterjee, S. & Datta, D. (1984). *An Introduction to Indian Philosophy.* Calcutta: University of Calcutta.

Dasgupta, S. N. (1940). *History of Indian Philosophy*. London: Cambridge University Press.

Dasgupta, S. N. (1991). *A History of Indian Philosophy: Reason and Enlightenment in the Tibetan Buddhism*. Delhi: Motilal Banarsidass.

Datye, V.H. (1954). *Vedanta Explained*. Mumbai: Book Sellers publishing Co.

Davids, C. A. (1900). A Buddhist manual of psychological ethics of the fourth century B.C. London: Royal Asiatic society.

Descartes, R. (2008). *Meditations*. New York: Cosimo Inc.

Foucault, M. (1999). *Religion and culture*. Manchester: Manchester University Press.

Gambhirananda, Swami (Tr.) (1965). *Brahma Sutra Bhashya of Shankarachrya*. Kolkota: Advaita Ashram.

Ganeri, A. (2003). *The Tipitaka and Buddhism*. Mankato: Black Rabbit Books.

Glasenapp, H. V. (1999). *Jainism: An Indian religion of salvation*. Delhi: Motilal Barasidass.

Goenka, S. N. (1987). *The Discourse Summaries*. Igatpuri: Vipassana Research Institute.

Harvey (1990). *Introduction to Buddhism*. Cambridge: Cambridge University Press.

Hawthorne, S. (2006). *Origins, Genealogies, and The Politics Of Identity: Towards a Feminist Philosophy Of Myth*. Unpublished PhD thesis, School of Oriental and African Studies, University of London.

Heidegger, M. (1962). *Being and time.* Oxford: Wiley-Blackwell.

Hirianna, M. (1918). *Outlines of Indian Philosophy.* London: George Allen and Unwin.

Hiriyanna, M. (2000). *Essentials of Indian Philosophy.*New Delhi: Motilal Banarsidas.

Hume, David (1817). *A treatise of human nature.* London: Oxford University.

Husserl, E. (1967). *The Paris lectures.* Norwell: Kluwer Academic Publishers.

Jaini, Padmanabh (1998). *The Jaina Path of Purification.* Delhi: Motilal Banarsidass.

Jantzen, G. (1998). *Becoming Divine: Towards a Feminist Philosophy of religion.* Bloomington: Indiana University Press.

Kant, I. (1781). *Critique of Pure Reason.* London: Cambridge University Press.

Kant, I. (1999). *Metaphysical elements of justice.* Indianapolis: Hackett Publishing

Karmarkar, R. D. (1966). *Sankara's Advaita.*Dharwar: Karnatak University.

Kramnick, I. (1995). *The Portable Enlightenment Reader.* London: Penguin.

Krishnamurti, J. & Bohm, David (1999). *The Limits of Thought: Discussions.* London: Routledge.

Krishnamurti, J. (1991). *The Collected Works of J. Krishnamurti, (1945-1948): The Observer Is the Observed.* Dubuque: Kendall/ Hunt Publishing Company.

Krishnamurti, J. (1992). *The Collected Works of J. Krishnamurti.* Ojai: Krishnamurti Foundation of America.

Krishnamurti, J. (1995). *The book of life: daily meditations with Krishnamurti.* San Francisco: Harper.

Krishnamurti, J. (2007). *The Collected Works of J. Krishnamurti.* Delhi: Motilal Banarasidass.

Lay, K. (1995). *Essence of Tipiṭaka.* Igatpuri: Vipassana Research Institute.

Mahadevan, T. M. P. (1959). *Ramana Maharshi and His Philosophy of Existence.* Thiruvannamalai: Sri Ramanasramam.

Mahadevan, T. M. P. (1969). *The Philosophy of Adviata.* Madras: Ganesh and Co.

Maharshi, R., Rāmānandasarasvatī, S. (1963). *Talks with Sri Ramana Maharshi..* Thiruvannamalai: Sri Ramanasramam.

Maharshi, B. S. R. (2006). *Origin of Spiritual Instruction.* Santa Cruz: Society of Abidance in Truth.

Maharshi, Ramana (1948). *Spiritual Instruction.* Thiruvannamalai: Sri Ramanasramam.

Maharshi, Ramana (1968). *Who am I?* Thiruvannamalai: T.N. Venkataraman.

Maharshi, Ramana (2004). *The Spiritual Teaching of Ramana Maharshi.* Boston: Shambhala.

Maharshi, Ramana (2005). *The teachings of Bhagavan Sri Ramana Maharshi in his own words.* Thiruvannamalai: Sri Ramanasramam.

Maharshi, Ramana. (1968). *Collected Works of Ramana Maharshi.* Thiruvannamalai: Sri Ramana Ashramam.

Mansfield, N. (2000). *Subjectivity: Theories of the Self from Freud to Haraway.* New York: New York University Press.

Max Müller, (tr.)(1962). *The Upanishads, (Part I & II).* New York: Dover Publications.

Müller, Friedrich Max (1900). *The Upaniṣads Sacred books of the East The Upaniṣads.* Oxford: Oxford University Press.

Murti, T.R.V. (1955). *The Central Philosophy of Buddhism.* London: George Allen and Unwin.

Muthuraman, M. (1976). *Outlines of vedantasara.* Madras: Muthuraman.

Nagendra Kr. Singh. (2001). *Encyclopedia of Jainism* (Edited by Nagendra Kr. Singh). New Delhi: Anmol Publications.

Nakamura, Hajime (2004), *A history of early Vedānta philosophy.* New Delhi: Motilal Banarsidass.

Nakamura, Hajime (2007). *Indian Buddhism (A Survey with Bibliographical Notes).* New Delhi: Motilal Banarsidass.

Narada. *The Buddha and his Teachings.* Kuala Lumpur: Buddhist Missionary Society.

Nietzsche, F. W. (1968). *Basic writings of Nietzsche.* New York: Modern Library.

Pandey, S.L. (1991). *Pre- Sankara Advaita Philosophy.* Alahabad: Darshana Pitha.

Plato (1997). *Complete Works.* Indianapolis: Hackett Publishing.

Plato (2001). *Alcibiades.* Cambridge: Cambridge University Press.

Plato (2009). *Collected Works of Plato.* Charleston: BiblioBazaar

Plato (2010). *Dialogues of Plato*.Cambridge: Cambridge University Press.

Prasad, Sital (1982). *A Comparative Study of Jainism and Buddhism.* Delhi: Sri Satguru Publications.

Radhakrishnan, S (1929). *Indian Philosophy, Volume 1.* London: George Allen and Unwin.

Radhakrishnan, S. (1994) [1953], *The Principal Upaniṣads.* New Delhi: HarperCollins.

Reddy, K. (2007). *Indian History.* New Delhi: Tata McGraw-Hill.

Rhys, Davids, T. W. (Ed. & Tr.) (1881) *Buddhist Suttas: Sacred Books of the East.* Oxford: Clarendon, reprinted by Delhi: Motilal Banarsidass.

Rose, D. (1995). *Buddhism.* Dublin: Folens Limited.

Sanghvi, S. (1974) (in trans. K. K. Dixit). *Tattvārthasūtra of Vācaka Umāsvāti.* Ahmedabad: L. D. Institute of Indology.

Sartre, J. (1957). *Existentialism and Emotions.* New York: Philosophical Library.

Scruton, R. (2001). *A short history of modern philosophy.* London and New York: Routledge.

Sharma, Arvind. (1993). *Experiential Dimension of Advaita Vedanta.* New Delhi: Motilal Banarsidass.

Sharma, B. N. (2000). *A history of the Dvaita school of Vedānta and its literature: from the earliest beginnings to our own times.* Delhi: Motilal Banarsidass.

Sharma, C. D. (1973). *A critical Survey of Indian Philosophy.* Varanasi: Motilal Banarasidass.

Sharma, C.D. (1996). *Advaita Tradition in Indian Philosophy*. Delhi: Motilal Banarasidass.

Siddhantacakravartin, N., Ghoshal, S. C. & Brahmadeva (1917). *Dravya-samgraha of Nemichandra Siddhanta-Chakravartti*. Delhi: Motilal Banarsidass.

Sinha, Jadunath (1952). *A history of Indian philosophy*. Calcutta: Sinha Publishing House.

Subhacandra, Nayavilāsa, & Shastri, B. (1977). *Jñānārṇava of Subhacandra*. Sholapur: JainaSaṃskrti Saṃrakshaka Saṅgha.

Tatia, Nathmal (2007). *Umasvati's Tattvartha Sutra - That Which Is*. Delhi: Motilal Banarsidass.

Tatia, Nathmal (tr.) (1994) (in Sanskrit - English). *Tattvārtha Sūtra: That which Is of Vācaka Umāsvāti*. Lanham: Rowman Altamira.

Thich Nhat Hanh (1974). *The Heart of the Buddha's Teaching*. New York: Broadway Books.

Varma, V. P. (2003). *Early Buddhism in Its Origins*. New Delhi: Munshiram Manoharlal.

Wijesekera, O.H.De A. & Jayasuriya, M.H.F. (Eds.). (1994) *Buddhist and Vedic Studies*. Delhi: Motilal Banarsidass.

Acknowledgements

Vijaya & Ashok Bhatewara,
Sadhvi Manjushri, St. Amitabh, Swami Amaranand Saraswati,
Dr Pradeep Gokhale, Udo Knipper

Organizations

Krishnamurti Foundations in India, America and England,
Sri Aurobindo Ashram, Auroville,
Sri Ramanashramam, Vipassana Research Institute,
Jain Shraman Sangh.
School of Oriental and African Studies, London;
Pune University

Linguistic

Alan Fahy, Priya Kothari, Dr Zara Ramsay

Visuals

Sadhana Bhagat, Isha Sonigra,
Shrishti Chatterjee, Jay

* 9 7 8 9 3 5 3 4 6 2 9 0 1 *